Radical Enfranchis... ... in the Jury Room and Public Life

Radical Enfranchisement in the Jury Room and Public Life

SONALI CHAKRAVARTI

The University of Chicago Press
Chicago and London

The University of Chicago Press, Chicago 60637

The University of Chicago Press, Ltd., London

© 2019 by The University of Chicago

Published 2019

Printed in the United States of America

28 27 26 25 24 23 22 21 20 19   1 2 3 4 5

ISBN-13: 978-0-226-65415-7 (cloth)

ISBN-13: 978-0-226-65429-4 (paper)

ISBN-13: 978-0-226-65432-4 (e-book)

DOI: https://doi.org/10.7208/chicago/9780226654324.001.0001

Library of Congress Cataloging-in-Publication Data:

Names: Chakravarti, Sonali, author.

Title: Radical enfranchisement in the jury room and public life / Sonali Chakravarti.

Description: Chicago ; London : The University of Chicago Press, 2019. | Includes bibliographical references and index.

Identifiers: LCCN 2018061748 | ISBN 9780226654157 (cloth : alk. paper) | ISBN 9780226654294 (pbk. : alk. paper) | ISBN 9780226654324 (e-book)

Subjects: LCSH: Jury—United States. | Jury duty—Political aspects—United States. | Jury nullification—United States.

Classification: LCC KF8972 .C53 2019 | DDC 345.73/075—dc23

LC record available at https://lccn.loc.gov/2018061748

♾ This paper meets the requirements of ANSI/NISO Z39.48-1992 (Permanence of Paper).

For Annika

CONTENTS

ACKNOWLEDGMENTS

I have benefited from the contributions of many peers in developing the ideas in this project, including those at the University Center for Human Values at Princeton University, the *Law's Mistakes* Seminar at Amherst College, the Wesleyan University-Chinese Academy of Social Sciences conference, the Tri-Co Political Theory Group, the University of Connecticut Political Theory Workshop, the Hunter College Workshop, the Law and Political Affairs (LAPA) workshop, the New School Political Theory Workshop, and the New York Legal Theory workshop. I am also lucky to know the following political theorists (and kindred scholars) "in real life," and I appreciate their insights: Ali Aslam, Yves Winter, Katherine Lemons, Youngjae Lee, Lida Maxwell, Turku Isiksel, Jennifer London, Melissa Schwartzberg, John McCormick, Bryan Garsten, Karuna Mantena, Austin Sarat, Leonard Feldman, Peter Brooks, Shatema Threadcraft, Alexander Hirsch, Kushanava Choudhury, D. Graham Burnett, and Albert Dzur. Neetu Khanna, Eirene Visvardi, and Supriya Kota provided fierce sisterly companionship. Don Moon was a steadfast mentor, and Seyla Benhabib's intellectual spirit influences these pages.

My love and gratitude to my parents, Rupali and Pradip Chakravarti, for encouraging my interests and making me feel like any path is possible, and to Devjit Chakravarti and Christina Royce for their encouragement. I want to celebrate this book with Sanford DeVoe, who went from friend to family during the course of writing it. Lastly, my heart is with Jac Mullen, who inspires me with his love and care every day.

In the final scene of *12 Angry Men*, Henry Fonda's character, the holdout juror who initially voices doubt about the murder charge and whose perspective triumphs in the end, is leaving the courthouse when he is approached by another juror.[1] The juror asks him, "What's your name?" "Davis," he responds. "My name's McCardle." The two part ways and slip into the streetscape, the credits roll. Throughout the film the men have been identified only by their juror numbers and, while morsels of personal information about jobs, families, and baseball teams have emerged, the two are essentially strangers. The moment when their identities are revealed seems largely insignificant; there is not a sense that they will become friends, but it highlights the jury room as a location distinct from all others we share with strangers in the capacities of judgment it demands, the solidarity that is possible, and the ethical weight of the task. Occupying the role of the juror requires a sharp break from the conventional ways one identifies oneself, beginning with one's name, and it should be seen as an opportunity to exercise an enhanced skill of judgment that includes taking responsibility for the treatment of fellow citizens and neighbors in a democracy. The current model for jury service is inadequate for this task, which requires a more focused and sophisticated form of civic education.

Juries have been at the center of some of the most emotionally charged moments of recent political life. In 2013 some Americans were outraged at the acquittal of George Zimmerman by a Florida jury for the shooting of Trayvon Martin; the outrage resurfaced with the 2014 decisions of two grand juries that did not indict police officers for the killings of unarmed black men. In this climate, juries and their capacity for legitimate decision-making have been under great scrutiny. These events have made it seem that the jury is both too powerful (when jurors fail to punish racially motivated violence) and too weak (completing a process that is rigged for or against certain defendants prior to the trial). This book suggests that the jury *could* be a forward-looking institution that nurtures the best democratic instincts of citizens, but this would require a change in education regarding the skills cultivated before and through the process of a trial. Being a juror, perhaps counterintuitively, can guide citizens in how to be thoughtful rule-breakers by changing their relationship to their own biases and by making options for collective action salient.

To those who are concerned that all this attention to the jury is misplaced because only a fraction of cases result in a jury trial (with the vast majority resolved through a guilty plea), I say, "Why care about love?" Juries, too, are fleeting and rare, but this only highlights their outsized importance in the legitimacy of the criminal justice system. The quest for love and the attempt to understand its mystery gives us insight into the values we cultivate in our interpersonal lives even if love is unrequited or thwarted. In a similar way, the standard of twelve peers deliberating about the appropriate degree, if any, of punishment is the regulatory ideal of the justice system. It shapes how laws are made, which charges are brought, and the range of sanctions we deem acceptable. Developing the skills of radical enfranchisement in potential jurors could benefit both defendants and jurors themselves. For defendants, renewed confidence in the jury trial could lead to a decline in guilty pleas by defendants who now feel coerced; for jurors, more active participation in the process may lead to knowledge about underutilized ways to shape the law and democratic norms, as well as greater faith in fellow citizens to be fair-minded, both shifts with profound political implications.

The *radical enfranchisement* of citizens is a type of political practice that goes beyond voting and demands that citizens navigate between desirable ends in the legal system, such as universalizability, fairness, retribution, mercy, and so on, each of which holds a place within the ideals of justice enshrined in the Constitution, case law, and collective memory. The adversarial criminal justice system is imbued with these principles; it is conceived of as a battle between opponents wherein each legal team appeals to the values that best suit their needs. As the arbiters of such a melee, each juror and the jury as a whole must ultimately come to a decision that reflects their perspective in a particular case.[2] Radical enfranchisement, as an ideal of citizenship, is promoted through increased civic education (such as with the Juror Project, described below) and then further developed via the structural aspects of the trial that mandate critical thinking and self-scrutiny. In both the jury room and public life, radical enfranchisement is a call for judgment by citizens that goes beyond obedience and rule-following in order to achieve justice and the emancipatory conditions of democracy. The common perception of jurors today is that they are not skillful enough to get out of jury duty and likely to be manipulated by attorneys who appeal to their most base prejudicial instincts. An orientation of radical enfranchisement works to upend these assumptions: jury service and the type of civic engagement that emerges from it demand that citizens are well-versed in their powers and responsibilities, able to scrutinize their own biases, and emboldened by the critical role they play in questions of punishment, a topic that is often understood to be formulaic and predetermined by convention (one that in the United States has come to mean consistently harsh sentences and an expectation that the criminal forfeits claims to humane treatment).[3] This process of education and jury service should lead to a type of practical wisdom necessary for identifying a just path for punishment, a skill valuable for political life but difficult to achieve.[4] In this way, the argument for radically enfranchised jurors should be seen as a third way in thinking about criminal justice, distinct from critics on the right who want harsh retributive sentences and believe that such consistency represents a desirable separation of law and politics, and those on the left who see the law as unable to foster any truly radical political program, regardless of what jurors know or do.

Enfranchisement, referring to the right to vote and to serve on a jury, is understood as the bedrock of civic participation but is not often thought of as particularly radical, a term saved for more revolutionary or rebellious acts directed outside of formal institutions. Its meaning is activated by precisely this tension: jurors who have an orientation of radical enfranchisement certainly hold institutional power, but they are aware that this does not imply obedience, technocratic applications of the law, or an affirmation of dogmatic prejudices, and this leads to a type of freedom often not found in institutional life. In addition, the fact that the jury is allowed to deliberate in private and without oversight makes the space one of unmatched possibility in changing the relationship of citizenship and punishment. Perhaps most controversially, radical enfranchisement entails that jurors understand the great discretion that they have within the criminal justice system, but discretion, "like the hole in a doughnut, does not exist except as an area left open by a surrounding belt of restriction. . . . It always makes sense to ask, 'Discretion under which standards?'"[5] The argument presented here clarifies the standards for discretion by jurors and the potential for justice that comes with its thoughtful execution.

Radical enfranchisement requires a more ambitious standard for civic education and is motivated by two sets of ideals: the first is accuracy in assessing evidence without recourse to bias; the second is a heightened appreciation for the authority jurors have to legitimate or deny punishment for the defendant as a decision distinct from their reflection on the evidence.[6] Allowing juries to run roughshod over the evidence to offer verdicts based on prejudicial opinions of the defendant (or the victim) fails the first ideal; outsourcing jury service to a judge for the sake of accuracy (a debatable premise) fails to meet the second. Together, these two ideals contribute to an understanding of justice that is more substantive than a defense based on procedural legitimacy and is asymptotically achieved through democratic deliberation about the remedy necessary in a given situation. Justice is thus always contextual, particular, and tied to ongoing duties of citizenship for both those who are punished and those who make the decisions.

In contrast to a view of justice that isolates *isonomia* (equality before the law) and places ultimate value in the consistency of retributive punishment, justice within the context of radical enfranchisement is better understood in the way the Roman jurist Ulpian described it: "the constant and perpetual will to render to each man his due."[7] The perpetual nature of the task is, in part, why the jury of laypeople, chosen by lot, is critical for the process. The demands on jurors are unrelenting in terms of time and attention and the stakes as high as they come for political life. To render each man his due, taking into account all the relative details, is a matter of virtue beyond the task of fidelity to the letter of the law.[8] Within the context of a more comprehensive civic education prior to service in the courtroom (in workshops or adult education courses, for example), potential jurors will learn not only about their responsibility for changing norms of punishment within the criminal justice system but also about alternatives to incarceration, including community mediation and restorative justice. Knowing the range of alternatives is necessary for meaningful consideration of what types of punishment and rehabilitation are appropriate given the democratic ideals to which the community aspires. These should not be questions considered for the first time during jury service, but rather should be part of an ongoing discussion within a community about the various iterations of self-governance that must include what happens when there are violations of the law. Those who are skeptical about jurors learning more about their responsibilities, including that of nullification, hope that ignorant jurors will stay close to the letter of the law, a desirable goal, but they do not recognize what is lost. It is through jury verdicts (and the education that precedes them) that communities come to have a better understanding of the ways the law and its application may be in flux—valuable information for diagnosing the subterranean fissures in the polity.

Radical enfranchisement as a transformative civic experience carries the potential to draw new lines of inclusion in ways that resist racial inequality. The current movement to end mass incarceration and stymie the democratically sanctioned economic and political incentives that have advanced it is challenging standards of punishment in a direct way, as are the efforts to question whether the collateral consequences of being designated a criminal (including the loss of voting rights, employment opportunities, eligibility for federal housing, etc.), are consistent with the tenets of democratic life.[9] It is the adjudication of punishment that provides the contours of what freedom means for citizens, and juries are a direct way for laypeople to be involved in this process, but they, lacking both civic education and motivation, have often avoided it. If the term "radical enfranchisement" were to have an (imprecise) antithesis, it might be felony disenfranchisement and the way in which citizenship is denied to those who have been declared guilty of the most serious criminal violations.[10] Just as felony disenfranchisement connotes the closing of both explicit channels of representation (voting) and implicit ones (the dignity and freedom afforded to citizens whose participation is valued), radical enfranchisement is a means to open up both explicit and implicit forms of emancipatory action for those able to recognize its significance.

The Juror Project, founded by William Snowden, a public defender in New Orleans, provides one model for what the radical enfranchisement of jurors may look like.[11] The project consists of workshops at high schools, community centers, and churches which highlight the importance of a diverse jury pool and the challenges of achieving it in the current jury system. Artfully weaving together simulations, Supreme Court cases, and anecdotes, Snowden is able to get a room full of people, tired after a long day at work, excited about jury service, and, more than that, able to see it as a part of a multifaceted strategy of activism, connected to the Movement for Black Lives and prison abolition. The workshop I attended took place at the Urban League in New Orleans: the audience was primarily black young professionals curious about the process of juror selection and the methods used to dissuade or remove blacks from serving. Snowden gave examples of the questions asked during voir dire and the strategies used by attorneys from both sides to ingratiate themselves with potential jurors; he also talked about the impact of nonunanimous verdicts, until recently acceptable in Louisiana, on the conviction rates in the state. One attendee asked how she could spread the word about juries (social media was his answer), another shared her experience of visiting a family member in prison who was later exonerated. She seemed to leave the workshop with renewed hope that a more diverse jury could reduce the number of false convictions and prevent others from going through the experience she had. The workshop was quite staid in its content and there was nothing that Snowden said that would have been out of place in a video shown to prospective jurors on the morning of jury duty—he did not speak about nullification, for example—but the energy of the room was palpable. There was a sense that a hidden form of democratic power was being made visible with consequences for all those who come into contact with the criminal justice system. It was a path of engagement through a morass that feels impenetrable.

The civic education that precedes the radical enfranchisement of jurors is a metacognitive endeavor, demanding that jurors pay attention to *how* they make decisions and not just the verdicts themselves. My argument for radical enfranchisement begins with an examination of how the political maturity of jurors within the criminal justice system is overlooked by one of its greatest proponents, Alexis de Tocqueville, at great cost to his analysis of democratic innovations. Then my project focuses on three key moments during the trial, each taken up in a chapter, where a change in the civic education of jurors can have a dramatic impact on the process. In each of three moments—(1) the conditions of a hung jury, (2) the examination of doubt, and (3) the possibility of jury nullification (where jurors give a verdict of not guilty as a result of the legitimacy of the law or their desire to show mercy to the defendant)—radically enfranchised jurors must put into practice skills of judgment and discernment while being acutely aware of the dangers of its misuse. The argument thus proceeds at two levels: (1) as an articulated set of skills and topics which jurors should be familiar with through civic education before a trial, and (2) as an orientation toward citizenship relevant for political life writ large that benefits from both pretrial education and the cognitive demands of a trial.[12] In conclusion, the last chapter examines several notable jury trials where a conceptual shift to radical enfranchisement could have affected the outcome. The chapter suggests that the deliberation in a jury room before the verdict is an important record of political and legal debate, though it is shrouded in secrecy. Still, enhanced education about what jurors should know and do could also serve as a forum for considering the buried history of jury deliberations. Through incorporating jury cases into our understanding of what can be considered just and appropriate punishment, we gain insight into the range of possibilities of punishment.

Enfranchisement on the Left and the Right

Two cases demonstrate what a jury may do if it has a heightened understanding of its role as an interpreter of law and is in possession of discretion regarding punishment. On August 22, 1971, a group of twenty-eight antiwar activists, including two Catholic priests and a Protestant minister, broke into the draft board office located on the fifth floor of the federal building in Camden, New Jersey.[13] There they attempted to destroy the paper records of all class 1-A draft registrants who had been cleared for unrestricted military service, but the attempt was foiled when they were caught by FBI agents, alerted to the plan by an informant active in the group. The participants were charged with seven felonies, including the destruction of government property and interfering with the Selective Service system. The judge allowed the defendants to explain their motivations, including their critique of actions undertaken by the US government in Vietnam and in Camden under the guise of urban renewal. The defense's argument was undeniably a political one in which the goal was to question the legitimacy of actions by the state in many domains—it was, in fact, a referendum on the war, and the jury was sympathetic. The jury in the Camden 28 trial seem to have understood that they were, indeed, the peers of the defendants and tasked with determining punishment through the verdict. While the judge explicitly told them not to nullify—the mere fact that this was discussed suggests a more expansive understanding of the jury than we traditionally see—they did not cower to his authority, one part of the enhanced power of the jury captured by radical enfranchisement. Radical enfranchisement would also have required an investigation into the biases that were affecting their decision.

In 2016 an Oregon federal jury found Ammon Bundy, along with his father, Cliven, and five codefendants not guilty on charges of conspiring to impede federal workers from entering the Malheur National Wildlife Refuge as well as on charges of possessing a firearm in a federal facility. The trial came after a six-week standoff at the refuge that resulted in the fatal shooting of a spokesperson for the occupation. While the prosecution was confident that the state had a strong case, Bundy and the other defendants claimed that the federal control of public lands was unconstitutional and was decimating the livelihoods of ranchers in the rural West. Theirs was a principled argument of disobedience, and it seemed to have traction with the jury, which issued a verdict of not guilty in what could be read as a nullification decision. The defendants may appreciate the framework of radical enfranchisement as consistent with their interests in amplifying the rights of self-determination for localities and resisting the overreach of the federal government through their actions in the courtroom. They may also interpret the verdict as an affirmation of their perspective as ordinary Oregonians who are concerned about the control of public land. Radical enfranchisement is thus not a Trojan horse for leftist political movements to achieve their agenda; it opens up the conversation about the application of the law and the society we want to achieve to jurors across the political spectrum with unpredictable results. The verdict in the Bundy case draws our attention to the depth of concern about land issues in a segment of the population that will undoubtedly use its collective will in other ways that have political implications.[14] We can either understand the verdict as a bell-wether of discontent to be taken seriously or discount it as an anomaly: in either case it provides democratic information necessary for developing the strategies of political parties and activists.

In light of these cases, one might be worried that the radical enfranchise-ment of jurors will lead only to acquittals, an outcome which could render criminal justice impotent, but this wrongly places an emphasis on outcome when radical enfranchisement is a commitment to process, especially the self-scrutiny required before one can adequately judge a case. Given that the system is currently experiencing a number of large-scale changes as govern-ment officials, prosecutors, and others try to dismantle the patterns that have allowed the law to be applied in racialized ways that have led to mass incarceration, a tendency to acquittal may be a necessary part of the process of change. At the same time, radical enfranchisement requires a commit-ment by citizens to take responsibility for punishment when it is warranted, with a clear understanding of the considerations and circumstances of the defendant—and this presents a different type of hard case than those that lead to jury nullification, but it requires an equally demanding set of skills that will be discussed in the following chapters, including an understanding of the purpose of unanimity and an interrogation of reasonable doubt.[15]

Radical enfranchisement as an attitude is also relevant for thinking about the interpersonal dynamics of jury deliberation, such as what might be ad-vantageous for jurors who find themselves approaching deadlock. Take, for example, Peggy, the juror described in Scott Sundby's investigation into jury deliberation during a capital punishment case in California.[16] She believed life without parole to be the appropriate punishment and was convinced that there were mitigating circumstances that should lead to the nonlethal option, but she lost the stamina to fight for this position after four days of being the target of questioning, skepticism, and the disdain of her fellow jurors. As the sole holdout, she did not have the fortitude to convince the others and, misinformed about what would happen if there were a hung jury (she thought it would automatically lead to the lesser sentence), felt that she could not, in good faith, precipitate that outcome. An orientation of radical enfranchisement might have nurtured in Peggy (1) confidence that her sense of the mitigating factors was consistent with her responsibilities as a juror; (2) the importance of anticipating and preparing for, to the best extent possible, the heated debate of the jury room; and (3) an understanding of the value of the hung jury.

A History of the Jury

Replacing the trial by ordeal, the modern jury trial emerged in the twelfth century with the incorporation of members of the community who could provide eyewitness accounts of the people in question during a criminal trial.[17] Through the Middle Ages, jurors continued to be selected for their direct knowledge, even when this required a *jury de mediatate lingua* or mixed jury, where half the jurors shared the linguistic or national identity of the defendant.[18] This right to a jury of true peers was also extended to defendants from specific guilds, such as the merchants, who would be better served with jurors who understood the conventions of their vocation. The jury design invoked for these cases prefigures contemporary discussions of what an impartial jury of one's peers should mean (in terms of racial or gender identity, for example) and the complexity of demanding that jurors be impartial while also valuing the specialized information that they may have.[19] Later, as the role of juror came to mean a neutral party who could act, in concert with others, as a check on the untrammeled power of the state, it took on an additional democratic valence. John Lilburne (1614–57), the Leveler leader opposed to Cromwell who thought that the law existed to protect the people's ability to exercise their freeborn rights, including the right not to self-incriminate, is known as one of the jury's most ardent supporters. A jury "freely chosen by the community" was included in the fundamental rights Lilburne articulated, and he put forth a defiant call to the jury to exercise its power in light of potent opposition from elites and political adversaries.[20]

The golden age of the jury in America can be traced to the colonial era where juries were a powerful voice in discussions of public interest at the local level and in dialogic relationship to judges and lawmakers.[21] Juries were expected to decide not just on the facts of a case but also on the interpretation of the law itself, including its legitimacy, relevance, and application to the conditions at hand.[22] The right of enfranchisement included being an active member of the jury no less than casting one's vote for representatives.[23] Radical enfranchisement builds on this conception of the jury even though the rise of a federalist state, with its hopes for the uniform application of the law and the valued contributions of a professional class, precipitated the dramatic decline of jury trials.[24] Changing norms and greater reliance on interpretations of physical evidence by police officers and judges in the nineteenth and twentieth centuries further cemented the deferential role of the jury to the officers of the court and the letter of the law, leading to a sharp increase in the percentage of cases settled by guilty plea by 1900.[25] The trend would only intensify. According the Bureau of Justice statistics, in 2009, nearly 97% of federal cases and 94% of state ones ended with no-contest or guilty pleas.[26] So few cases go to jury today that judges report sitting on the bench for several years without ever presiding over a jury trial; plea bargaining agreements have come to reign supreme, completely removing the role of laypeople from the process.[27] Albert Altschuler disputes interpretations that defend the rise of plea bargains as inevitable, and he highlights the distinction between the long-standing tradition of providing an incentive for the accused to give information to the state and providing an incentive for the accused to self-incriminate.[28] The latter challenges the integrity of the criminal justice system and should be the object of criminal justice reforms, but a decline in plea bargains is difficult to achieve due to desires for expediency and cost-effectiveness on the side of the state and a risk-averse orientation held by the defendant who exists in a society where misdemeanor charges are legion (and can be used to increase potential punishments). While the right to a trial by a jury is enshrined in the Sixth and Seventh Amendments, along with the final authority of a jury decision, jury service has become a rare occurrence and is no longer celebrated as an important democratic adjudication of the tension between justice and the letter of the law.[29]

Democracy, for Sheldon Wolin, requires temporal interruption of the constitutional bulwarks of institutional politics—these are necessary "fugitive" acts.[30] Over time, the deep fear of instability and of mass control held by elites becomes entrenched in political institutions and creates norms that close off the enfranchisement of citizens, even in republics that were founded on its expansion. It is this contradiction between the *raison d'état* of expanded political participation and the consolidated workings of the state that leads to a convulsive pattern of stasis and revolution. Fugitive democracy consists of the events and ideas that disrupt the stasis.[31] The criminal justice system may be a quintessential case of an institution "devitalized by form," but the jury, while still located within a formal institution, has its own form of fugitive power in its ability to render verdicts that recast notions of what justice means at a particular moment. Jason Frank's concept of constituent moments, "when the underauthorized—imposters, radicals, self-created entities—seize the mantle of authorization, changing the inherited rules of authorization in the process" further captures how creative action within an institution can be radical in spirit and thus activate an enlarged notion of citizenship that continues to influence everyday politics.[32] Jurors are the authors of justice, not just its minions, but the fact that their power is vested with institutional protections has often obscured its radical potential to interrupt ossified practices of citizenship, even for scholars who may be predisposed toward such actions.

On Populism

Radical enfranchisement is distinct from the type of resentment-driven populism surging in liberal democracies today because of its belief in both the integrity of institutions and the civic benefits gained from participating in those institutions. Although radical enfranchisement may be understood as antielitist in orientation, it is not making a moral claim about the true identity of the people, nor the impossibility of a pluralist vision of democratic life, tropes of the populist phenomena.[33] The variant of populist sentiment most commonly tied to criminal justice is what John Pratt calls "penal populism," which may appear to share with radical enfranchisement enthusiasm about increased citizen engagement on questions of punishment and sentencing.[34] Yet, penal populism, often measured by popular opinion, is driven by a sense that entire (frequently racially and socioeconomically specific) communities should be seen as victims of criminal behavior and that their rights must take precedence over the rights of individual criminals; the justice system is, in their view, too soft on crime.[35] Jurors who feel this way may in fact be harder on defendants than judges, suggesting that greater civic participation does not necessarily mean leniency.[36] A retributivist orientation finds expression through voting and political campaigns, with referenda for stricter sentencing guidelines, for example, rather than in the extensive deliberation that can go on in trial, where jurors are expected to heed several parameters to insure that the rights of the individual defendants are protected. Penal populism is often reduced to sloganeering ("three strikes and you're out" may be the best example) and the performative spectacle of legislators and citizens denouncing criminality and the irresponsibility that emerges from it. In contrast, radical enfranchisement calls on jurors to understand the gravity and particularity of each case and, more importantly, to go through the self-scrutiny and deliberation required to take responsibility for their decisions as consistent with the democratic process and the best hope for justice.[37] Albert Dzur has drawn a distinction between thin and thick populism that captures these key differences; while thin populism (like penal populism) focuses on distrust of an intrusive and coercive government, often from a homogenous citizen base, thick populism sees the potential for institutional reform and the building of capacity through greater participation in projects of the commonwealth.[38]

Radical Enfranchisement and the Rule of Law

The vision of justice described here is in tension with what is often called the "rule of law," a normative ideal of the authority of the legal code and its institutions as the critical check on unbridled tyranny, including that of the people. The tenet that laws, not men, should govern is thought to be the best hope for treating individuals equally, without prejudice or political malice, and creating a sense of continuity and fairness with respect to the norms of collective life. Robert Burns has fruitfully described the "received view of trial," the ideal type of a trial within a rule of law framework, as aiming to achieve the following benefits: the trial should (1) reflect substantive legitimacy, (2) prevent the abuse of power by individual government actors, (3) allow citizens a level of control over the time and place the coercive engines of government may be brought to bear, and (4) best ensure that similar cases will be treated similarly.[39] I do not deny that each of these is a benefit of the trial and important for democratic life, but there are cases when other values become salient and the jury should be prepared to recognize them—which is currently impossible given the information available to citizens about their role in punishment.[40] To say that the rule of law approach is not desirable in certain cases might be both obvious, given the many realms of human sociability that respect alternate modes of judgment, and startling, in that it seems to invite a politicization of punishment that could eventually result in anarchic chaos. Moreover, one might argue that shoring up the rule of law is the ubiquitous challenge for political life, in light of corruption, racism, oligarchic power, and so on, and, as such, it dwarfs other complementary concepts for juries that might warrant attention. Yet, the concept of radical enfranchisement elucidates how a rule of law approach to understanding the jury is shortsighted, compromising the institution in a way that is inconsistent with its function and squandering the opportunity to redefine the relationship between the work of citizenship and the reflection that must precede decisions regarding punishment.

Jacques Rancière, concerned with the twin problems of rule by coercion and rule by experts in a managerial state that purports to be pursuing consensus, gives another reason for the centrality of lay decision-making when he puts forth a theory of politics as one of surplus, "making visible what has no reason to be seen."[41] A politics of surplus is also dependent on the perspectives of those whose absence has been definitive of the demos.[42] In fact, drawing on the qualifications for governing set forth by Plato in *Laws* (690e), democracy is "characterized by the drawing of lots, or the complete absences of any entitlement to govern."[43] While Rancière uses the ideal of sortition to highlight politics as a rupture in the conventional techniques of governance, he also provides a potential interpretation of the jury, chosen by lot and inclusive of those who do not otherwise hold significant legal or political power.[44] The fact that the critical decision about punishment in a democratic state hinges on the verdict of those who are traditionally not entitled to govern captures the dynamism necessary for politics to not devolve into coercion and technocracy. To be chosen by lot echoes the loss of conventional labels of identity portrayed in *12 Angry Men*; one is selected as a juror by virtue of chance, not merit or status, and this foregrounds the opportunity to relate to the defendant and fellow citizens in ways closed off by the strictures of identity. To see the possibilities of radical enfranchisement in sortition does not imply that all jurors, just by virtue of service, will leave with an enhanced conception of civic participation. They may have been "forced to be free" in the Rousseauian sense but may not have had the (1) foreknowledge about the power of the jury, (2) self-scrutiny about their own biases, or (3) awareness of the opportunities to exercise this freedom; radical enfranchisement is never inevitable.

The centrality of laypeople, those not trained in the law, to the work of punishment is arguably a counterintuitive proposition, especially if the hope is to restructure punishment in light of the debilitating consequences of mass incarceration.[45] Even among democratic political theorists, an actuarial or expert-led approach to determining punishment, such as through the use of sentencing policy boards (separate from parole boards), has its proponents and raises the question, "Why are juries of laypeople preferable to legal experts in determining guilt?"[46] While others have put forth an answer based on collective wisdom as a way to mitigate bias and make use of different forms of expertise, this is not the primary motivation for radical enfranchisement.[47] Rather, it prioritizes the jury as a check on the closed, elite-led processes of the state at the point of the state's greatest power, that is, in the moments before punishment is made legitimate. It is not that laypeople are always more accurate (although research shows that there is convergence in verdicts between juries and judges approximately 80% of the time), but that defendants deserve a jury of their peers at the time of judgment because state-sanctioned violence is at stake.[48] The potential severity of the outcome adds a layer of gravity to the task of judgment about punishment that demands the undivided attention of a group of citizens who will not find it banal. As G. K. Chesterton wrote:

> And the horrible thing about all legal officials, even the best, about all judges, magistrates, barristers, detectives, and policemen, is not that they are wicked (some of them good), not that they are stupid (several of them are quite intelligent), it is simply that *they have got used to it.* Strictly they do not see the prisoner in the dock; all they see is the usual man in the usual place. They do not see the awful court of judgment: they only see their own workshop.[49]

Ironically, it is Hobbes who had an acute understanding of the critical role a jury of laypeople plays even in the most autocratic of regimes. He writes, "In like manner, in the ordinary trials of Right, Twelve men of the common People, are the Judges, and give Sentence, not only of the Fact, but of the Right." The power of the interpretation of laws is the ultimate act of sovereignty in a political regime that looks to no external source for validation, including natural law. In Hobbes's view, the jury should hold this power as a necessary check on the Leviathan, making them not only triers of fact but also of the law itself and of the validity of sanction by force.

In comparing the rule of law understanding of the trial with radical enfranchisement, there appears to be disagreement over the preferred relationship between law and politics. To those who say that the ideal of the rule of law starkly separates the two, I would question the genealogy of such a claim.[50] It is the political framework that gives meaning to the rule of law and, in the language of Carl Schmitt, designates the sovereign as he who has the power to decide on the exception to (legal) norms.[51] The penumbra of the rule of law does thereby not necessarily extend to those who hold political power, even in the context of institutions purportedly built around such a logic. Furthermore, to suggest that invoking the rule of law is a neutral value with regards to political power is to engage in a political act in itself, functioning to draw attention to the illusion of equality under the law in order to obscure other conflicts.[52] In nonideal regimes, the encroachment of political will on the rule of law is taken to be a symptom of dysfunctionality or the unfulfilled potential of the rule of law; these interpretations are not wrong, but even in its ideal form there are unresolvable tensions. In light of these immanent challenges to the purity of the legal-political dyad embedded in the rule of law perspective, an orientation of radical enfranchisement should be understood as a variation on the relationship between law and politics, rather than its inversion, and one that delegates to jurors the Schmittian moment of sovereignty that legitimates exception. Radical enfranchisement takes as its premise that the institution of the jury, a deliberate fracture in the edifice of a closed, technocratic, administrative process, is sui generis in what it demands in relation to both law and politics. Jurors must adhere to institutional norms in a far more demanding way than they have to in voting, the other pole of enfranchisement, yet it is not their purpose to serve solely as legal functionaries. The jury is also sui generis in the kinds of conversations it demands we have with strangers. While some jurors will be more vocal than others, none can opt out of the process of judgment. Every vote always counts in a jury.

The claim that justice in the eyes of a jury goes beyond the received view of the trial might best be understood by thinking about radical enfranchisement as a practice. Drawing on the Aristotelian lineage of the concept and Alasdair MacIntyre's influential interpretation of it, a practice is a collective, complex enterprise that connects practitioners over time with internally derived standards of excellence.[53] Other components that emerge when thinking about radical enfranchisement as a practice include the goal of developing a type of practical wisdom (*phronesis*) within the legal context that is distinct from merely knowing legal jargon or relying on folk wisdom, the need to repeatedly encounter key concepts over time, cultivating the intrinsic motivation of those who participate, a heightened sense of the role-playing attached to being a juror, public discussion of what makes jury decisions better or worse, and a community of people concerned with the integrity of the practice, beginning perhaps with civics teachers and including community activists, concerned citizens, and members of the legal community.[54] The received view of jury service includes a standard of excellence in relation to unbiased consideration of the evidence and the reasonable doubt standard (concerns that overlap with the ideals of radical enfranchisement), but it has often not included attention to the critical moment of the verdict as a separate judgment about punishment, one that is closely connected to the jury as a political check on the judge, attorneys, and lawmakers.

It is well documented that jury pools are skewed such that racial minorities are dramatically underrepresented, especially in trials where the defendant is from a minority group.[55] This is due not only to the difficulty of stopping the practice of race-based dismissal as Batson violations, but also in the very procedure used to generate the venire that favors those who are registered to vote, have driver's licenses, and maintain the same address over time.[56] The 2016 Supreme Court decision in *Foster v. Chatman* made it clear that blatant, well-documented attempts to prevent citizens from serving on a jury because of their race cannot be justified, but most cases are not so easily assessed; much more needs to be done, including an end to peremptory challenges altogether, the enfranchisement of formerly convicted people, and the use of residential lists for the venire, to ensure that juries truly reflect the populations from which they are selected.[57] For the radical enfranchisement of jurors to matter, there must be major reforms in how jurors are selected.

In making the move from the jury room to public life, radical enfranchisement entails taking the skills of assessment, self-scrutiny, and deliberation that were forged in the crucible of the criminal trial and applying them to questions of citizenship and punishment in political life. Let's compare jury service to softball: playing softball requires knowing the rules of the game, working with a team, and developing the skills of hitting, pitching, catching, running, and so on. It is a distinct endeavor with its own constraints, yet training for softball would be beneficial when playing other sports, especially bat-and-ball sports, and may increase the likelihood of participating in them. The physical fitness required to play softball and the knowledge one gains about how such sports work would carry over to other athletic events, in both conscious and unconscious ways, including the self-confidence one has in one's abilities and the esteem one has for others who play the game. The relationship between the radical enfranchisement of jurors to their role in political life is analogous—it improves the fitness of jurors for the tasks of democracy.

James Forman's research on how black law enforcement officers and judges, including police officers and prosecutors, participated in the high rates of black incarceration in the last three decades provides an insight relevant for thinking about the role of juries.[58] He argues that class bias and an admixture of fatigue, frustration, and despair led black officers of the law as well as political officials to pursue policies of "locking up their own." Such an observation suggests that a more racially representative jury may not necessarily be more amenable to greater compassion for the defendant. These juries might end up being punitive and discriminatory in their own way and for the sake of an imagined community. Still, Forman is hopeful that officials and citizens could ideally consider alternatives for defendants that emphasize accountability without vengeance, including "pretrial diversion programs to funnel people into drug treatment instead of prisons, funding public defenders adequately, giving discretion back to judges by eliminating mandatory minimums, building quality schools inside juvenile and adult prisons, restoring voting rights to people who have served their sentences, and welcoming—not shunning and shaming—those who are returning from prison."[59] While jurors are not responsible for these decisions, their familiarity with them will have an impact on how they understand the relationship between the rule of law and justice; incarceration is not the only way to communicate that a norm has been broken or to deter others from committing a crime. Furthermore, if a jury does not return with a guilty verdict, it may not mean that they condone the action or think the defendant should never be held accountable, but that there are other approaches to achieve that end. Yet, to make these types of differentiated decisions about punishment and the exercising of democratic norms, a new framework for understanding juror responsibility and discretion is necessary.

The Case for Radical Enfranchisement

Virtually any historical discussion of the American jury begins with Tocqueville's admiration of the institution during his famous trip of 1831. Tocqueville is often celebrated for recognizing the pedagogical function of the jury, but I will argue that his vision has serious constraints on how autonomous jurors should be. Chapter 1 argues that Tocqueville understands how the intervention of jurors can mitigate some of the deficiencies of democracy, but he does not encourage them to fully realize this potential—their maturity, like that of women, is always in question. His sense of moderation regarding the republican virtue of participation and his admiration for aristocratic leadership make it impossible for him to cultivate the ideal of jurors as radically enfranchised citizens providing some of the best arguments for the value of their political interventions.

The declaration of a hung jury is one of the most dramatic moments in the legal process. All of the resources and efforts invested in a trial can be perceived to have been for naught when a jury expected to reach a unanimous verdict (either guilty or not guilty) fails to do so. For the defendant, a hung jury may be celebrated as a brief reprieve—there will be another trial or pressure to plea bargain from the state, but it is significant that a jury of one's peers did not find the evidence adequately convincing. For the prosecution, the hung jury is likely felt as a waste of time and money. Chapter 2 examines whether or not the hung jury should be understood as a mistake, that is, an outcome that reveals a breakdown in the procedures of the trial or undermines the tenets of the adversarial justice system. The hung jury is a sanctioned option within US law, so it should not be seen as an aberration, but the mixed reactions to it suggest further consideration of the jury process and obstacles to consensus. An orientation of radical enfranchisement also suggests that jurors should understand the stakes of a failure to reach consensus but also the ways such an outcome demonstrates the function of the jury system as a microcosm of democratic decision-making.

"Reasonable doubt," a term that seems to lose clarity as it is further defined, demands that jurors assess what they know, what they don't, and what they could never know. Chapter 3 first examines the reasonable doubt standard in American legal history as it has evolved over time. Debates over its meaning offer clues as to what may be required for radical enfranchisement as both an ethical and an intellectual orientation contra "doxa," Roland Barthes's term for the assumptions that go unquestioned within society. While applying the reasonable doubt standard to the prosecutorial evidence is the primary way of understanding it, I suggest that it is also a useful way for jurors to scrutinize their own biases. They must bring a sense of reasonable doubt to the shortcuts and instinctual reactions that may be dominating their judgment about the case. This internalization of doubt is aided by an awareness of implicit bias, the allure of narrative closure, and a renewed understanding of the presumption of innocence. Taken together these conventions demonstrate the way that the institutional structure of the trial facilitates a type of critical thinking that can be carried over to political life.

In Chapter 4 I shift my focus to those who are deeply suspicious of the criminal justice system because of racialized violence and I consider the value of the jury for them. In particular, I place jury nullification—the jury's use of discretion to render not guilty verdicts—alongside more radical measures that usher in new ways of thinking about the law. I build on work by Kadish and Kadish to theorize the jury in terms of its role as marked by the possibility of "legitimate interposition."[60] While others may argue that jurors must either be bound to the conventions of legal decision or act only as they deem best in the service of justice, they suggest that the role of the juror is to fully inhabit both positions.[61] While over two hundred years of American jurisprudence actively rehearses the dialogue between those who argue that jurors should be judges of fact and the law and those who do not, nullification remains a secret.[62] The final part of chapter 4 considers the thought-experiment of a three-option verdict: *guilty, not guilty, nullify* as a way to end the secrecy and examine what radical enfranchisement might look like in difficult cases, taking into account the dual needs of impartial deliberation about the evidence and reflection on the appropriateness of punishment in the case. Having the three-option verdict would prompt discussion about the use of mercy and discretion in the criminal justice system, thus enhancing and emboldening the work of activists who aim to transform the criminal justice system in fundamental ways.[63]

William Penn, the defendant in a trial that would become one of the most famous in jury history because of the jury's perceived defiance, wrote a personal transcript of the trial as part of his book, *The People's Ancient and Just Liberties Asserted*. He defended liberty of conscience, protection for religious assembly, and support for the jury as a robust defense against corrupt judges and elites willing to abuse their power. His use of the trial to demonstrate the practice of liberty allowed Penn to foreground the performative and nonverbal aspects of political life.[64] Radical enfranchisement brings back that sensibility as it sees the jury as an important node in the expansion of political theory from below. Jurors not only witness the back-and-forth of the adversarial relationship in the court and their relationship to the judge but also must navigate disagreements during deliberation. Some of these disagreements will be factual or legal, but some will concern what constitutes fair punishment and whether imprisonment is appropriate, critical questions of political life. Chapter 5 examines several jury trials where skills consistent with radical enfranchisement were evident, or badly needed, as jurors demonstrated how greater awareness of the scope of their role might have been useful for their task. For example, examining the cases of Cecily McMillan, the Occupy Wall Street activist charged with assaulting a police officer, reveals the discomfort jurors have with not knowing the sentencing guidelines for the charges. Alternatively, the case of the antiwar activists breaking into a Camden, New Jersey, draft board office during the Vietnam era elucidates what a transformed view of punishment might look like for future civil disobedience cases, especially those where the state employed an informant.

Radical enfranchisement seeks to reconsider jury service through making education and preparation for it more robust through workshops like the Juror Project. It seeks to clarify the tasks of jurors both in relation to their own biases and their responsibility for punishment. It has been assumed that the lottery process for jury service necessitates getting jurors with a dearth of knowledge about the process, but what if we envisioned jury service as a critical event in political life and trained citizens accordingly?

That political philosophy (through the trial of Socrates) and Christianity (through the trial of Jesus) both take trials as their founding moments suggests that it is perhaps through the act of being jurors that we come to understand the clash of underlying values which govern our lives. Abstract conceptions about punishment and human nature are made manifest in a trial when the threat of violence by the state is real and the alternative path of acquittal is plain to see. In the context of a trial, jurors must not only be attentive to the conflicting patterns of fact and value that the two sides present and the aporias in meaning that emerge, they must also summon the courage to judge.

ONE

Mature Enough to Disobey: Jurors, Women, and Radical Enfranchisement in Tocqueville's *Democracy in America*

I do not, then, assert that all the members of the legal profession are at all times the friends of order and the opponents of innovation, but merely that most of them are usually so. In a community in which lawyers are allowed to occupy without opposition that high station which naturally belongs to them, their general spirit will be eminently conservative and anti-democratic. When an aristocracy excludes the leaders of that profession from its ranks, it excites enemies. . . . But whenever an aristocracy consents to impart some of its privileges to these same individuals, the two classes coalesce very readily and assume, as it were, family interests.

—Alexis de Tocqueville, *Democracy in America*

Any argument celebrating the distinctive legal and political role American juries play evokes a reference to Tocqueville's observations during his 1831 trip. While many have pointed to Tocqueville's admiration of the jury system as a schoolhouse for civic participation, I will argue that Tocqueville sets up, but forgoes, the opportunity to make jurors empowered enough to counter the ills of democracy he also enumerates. His sense of moderation regarding the republican virtue of participation and his admiration for aristocratic leadership make it impossible for him to cultivate the ideal of jurors as radically enfranchised citizens, meaning those who have an understanding of the weight and expectations of legal judgment but are also able to challenge the authority of the law in certain instances, such as via jury nullification (the undisclosed power a jury has to find a defendant not guilty because they find the law itself objectionable). As a way to explore both Tocqueville's celebration of the jury for its democratic value, and then his hamstringing of its power, I turn to an analysis of his perception of the education of girls in American society. By juxtaposing two sections of *Democracy in America* that are normally thought of separately, I will show that, in the case of both jurors and women, Tocqueville falters in his perception of their enfranchisement while also providing some of the best arguments for the value of their political interventions.

The right to a trial by jury is enshrined in the Sixth Amendment of the Constitution: "In all criminal prosecutions, the accused shall enjoy the right to a speedy and public trial, by an impartial jury of the state and district wherein the crime shall have been committed, which district shall have been previously ascertained by law, and to be informed of the nature and cause of the accusation; to be confronted with the witnesses against him; to have compulsory process for obtaining witnesses in his favor, and to have the assistance of counsel for his defense."[1] Later case law established that juries in lower courts must have at least six persons and be unanimous in their decision while federal criminal juries require twelve.[2] A jury that cannot reach unanimity is considered to be a hung jury (and the occasion for a mistrial) and provides grounds for a new trial should the prosecution choose to proceed. At the state and local levels, the specific procedures for juries may vary but the essence remains the same: an impartial jury of citizens determines whether the state has met the burden of proof for establishing guilt. The specification of the jury trial in the Constitution alongside other rights of the accused confirms this defendant-protecting value of a jury. In contrast to an inquisitorial system in which the state acts as prosecutor, investigator, and arbiter, the adversarial model demands that the defendant have an array of protections of which the trial by jury is one.

The American Jury through the Eyes of a Frenchman

Coming to the United States in part to study the penal system, Tocqueville was particularly attuned to how the people he encountered—judges, lawyers, farmers, doctors among them—understood the legal process. While he was more drawn to how the culture of American life allowed democracy to exist without a descent into mob violence, he also accounted for institutional considerations. The most important of these was and still is the Constitution and the authority it continues to have in legal and political life; it is responsible, along with civic culture, for preventing both the despotism of the elite and the unqualified sovereignty of the people through the balance of power it articulates and the codification of individual liberties. He saw that it was the Constitution that provides a shared understanding of justice and that it was necessary to curtail competing transcendent ideals that masqueraded as justice but resulted in terror. As such, Tocqueville's appreciation of the Constitution closely fit with his sense that democracy, with all its flaws and attractions, was a historical inevitability and that France's experience with the transition to a constitutional republic was too violent but unavoidable. His task was not to persuade or dissuade his readers of democracy's normative desirability but rather to observe how its American instantiation was surviving, both in the everyday lives of its citizens and the robustness of its legal and political institutions.

At first glance one would think that a discussion of juries in the political process and the independence of women would be unrelated, but by looking at the concept of political maturity we see that these two concerns are deeply linked in Tocqueville's work. While radical enfranchisement is a way of thinking about political participation applicable to all, it is particularly salient for groups that have been denied a standing of political maturity, that is, forced to occupy a liminal space between adolescence and the equality and respect given to fully autonomous citizens. This liminal space is social, intellectual, and ethical, and while there may be fears about the impact of a demos truly composed of politically mature subjects, there should also be fears about the consequences of a legal system that perpetuates stunted development. Perceptions of women's political immaturity stem largely from cultural and social norms embedded in a variety of relationships; the relative narrowness of the role of the juror provides a helpful contrast that elucidates the lost possibility for radical enfranchisement. Jurors in Tocqueville's account, I will argue, *partially* realize how important they are as a check on the power of the political and legal elite, but are not empowered enough to use this power in the most challenging circumstances. Women may be both less aware of the critical function they play and may perceive only insurmountable obstacles to enfranchisement.

At the beginning of the section on the jury, Tocqueville celebrates its republican character and its prominence as an instrument of popular participation, but remarks that he is more concerned with its political rather than legal impact. In his words:

> By the jury I mean a certain number of citizens chosen by lot and invested with a temporary right of judging. Trial by jury, as applied to the repression of crime, appears to me an eminently republican element in the government, for the following reasons. The institution of the jury may be aristocratic or democratic, according to the class from which the jurors are taken; but it

always preserves its republican character, in that it places the real direction of society in the hands of the governed, or of a portion of the governed, and not in that of the government.[3]

Just as with universal suffrage, with the final decision-making power of juries, power is truly in the hands of the people, with all of their foibles. While such power could make some feel ill at ease, Tocqueville's use of the language of republicanism, with its connotation of participation and self-rule, indicates an unexpected enthusiasm for such a mechanism of democracy in a situation of stark importance. When he mentions the aristocratic possibility within juries he suggests that jurors' existing orientations to privilege, hierarchy, and tradition are already ingrained before they take on their civic responsibility. Nonetheless, Tocqueville is highlighting that even when it is made up of a subgroup of the elite, the jury represents a substantial check on other expressions of power.

Tocqueville famously described juries as "a school, free of charge and always open, where each juror comes to be instructed in his rights and comes into communication with the most instructed and enlightened members of the upper classes, where the laws are taught to him in a practical manner and are put within reach of his intelligence by the efforts of the attorneys, the advice of the judge, and the passions of the parties."[4] Tocqueville considers French discussions about the standards for intelligence necessary for jury service to be misguided because of this pedagogical function of juries. To fixate on the cognitive ability any given juror brings to the process is to miss the point—jury service is itself a form of education and a type of treatment for inchoate citizens. Yet, within his description of the jury as schoolhouse, there is both a sense of ambition about what laypeople acting as a jury can achieve and of paternalism manifested in the hope that they follow the expertise of court officials. Tocqueville seems to see these different qualities of the "schoolhouse" as mutually reinforcing; interaction with the elite and with the law can be complementary to interaction with fellow jurors. Education, while transformative, also requires that one accept the limited autonomy of the student. The knowledge of rights, individually and as a collective, is not meant to ever challenge the interests of the court; Tocqueville is hopeful about the potential for harmony between the jury and the necessarily aristocratic elements of the court and its officers, a type of nobility he purports to be useful in democratic societies.

Tocqueville's celebration of the opportunity for lay (including nonelite) participation on juries and his hope that they might be positively influenced by those who are the "most enlightened members of the upper classes" captures a contemporary tension in thinking about jury life. Even as he remarked on the importance of taking into account the insights of ordinary people as a check on centralized power and the potential misuse of legal statutes, he still harbored a belief in the wisdom of the officers of the court and the assumption that laypeople should aspire to be more like them. This position is most clearly seen in his depiction of the civil jury, the place where the jury has the most influence in shaping social norms and the national character. On the stature of the judge in a civil case, Tocqueville explains, "The jurors view him with confidence, and they listen to him with respect; for here his intelligence entirely dominates theirs. . . . His influence over them is almost boundless."[5] The power of the jury is thus, in Tocqueville's estimation, a power given with one hand and pulled back with the other. Saving the people from themselves while at the same time encouraging them to use the distinctive power that they have is at the crux of the Tocquevillian defense of juries. The argument for radical enfranchisement is more specific about the importance of jury power at exceptional moments of disagreement, particularly when a jury refuses to be led by the aristocratic elements of the court.[6]

It is tempting to attribute Tocqueville's comment about the wisdom jurors gain from elites to his affinity for aristocratic regimes and a corresponding nostalgia for the stability ensured by such regimes. While his concern with stability is important for understanding the constraints he places on the political maturity of juries, Tocqueville is too nuanced a thinker and too honest about the flaws of each regime he considers to make such a reductionist claim about aristocracies and stability. Moreover, his insights about the manner in which aristocratic regimes crumble are helpful for thinking about juries. In describing the causes of the French Revolution, he places some of the blame on the monarchy's willingness to destroy long-standing institutions and wield its own violent power. He writes, "When the people saw the parlement, almost as old as the monarchy and which had seemed up to then as unshakable as it was, fall and disappear, and [they] vaguely understood that we were approaching those times of violence and chance when everything becomes possible, when there is nothing so old that it must be respected, nor so new that it may not be tried."[7] It is thus not aristocracy itself that contains a heightened understanding of the fragility of peace and the value of traditional institutions. Kings as well as revolutionaries are seduced by the allure of the new.

The legal arbitrariness of the old regime, in particular the utter disenfranchisement of a poor citizen who had a grievance with the state, was also compelling to Tocqueville as one of the ways in which the old regime sowed the seeds of its own destruction. Arrests without warrants, prolonged detention without charge, farcical trials—these commonplace occurrences in the old regime provided, in Tocqueville's assessment, a blueprint for revolutionary action. In a wry comment that stands in parallel to the way Tocqueville describes juries as "schoolhouses" for democracy, he writes, "It is thus that a mild and well-established government daily taught the people the code of criminal justice most appropriate to revolutionary periods and best adapted to tyranny. *Its school was always open*. The old regime gave this dangerous education to the poorest of the poor."[8] The fact that the mores of the old regime were not enough to prevent it from the excesses of tyrannical oversight and corruption suggests the need for a legal code committed to the protection of individual rights. Even regimes committed to excellence, tradition, and stability, as the best aristocratic ones are, can unravel in this particular way. In addition to the need for individual rights that emerges from Tocqueville's depiction, there is also a need for counterelite checks within the legal system, and this insight is immanent within his writings on the old regime. It is not just that the poor do not have rights, but also that their interests are different from those of the elite (and from those of the middle class), and Tocqueville provides a foundation for thinking about the jury as a place where such divergences are given formal recognition.

While the Constitution is the blueprint for questions of justice, the role of interpretation is again left to fallible individuals. In considering the role of judges in relation to the law, Tocqueville points to the accumulated power of judicial censure. "Now, on the day when the judge refuses to apply a law in a case, at that instant it loses a part of its moral force. Americans have therefore entrusted an immense political power to their courts; but in obliging them to attack the laws only by judicial means, they have much diminished the dangers of this power."[9] The superiority of the legislative process over the judiciary is thus preserved with judicial review, in Tocqueville's mind, because the judicial branch can express its will in bounded ways—law by law, case by case—and thereby the constitutionality and the weight of circumstances can be tested episodically in the courtroom without a direct attack on authority. Such a perception about the importance of piecemeal and interpretive work should also carry over to jury decisions that may not be in line with what officers of the court would like. Tocqueville does not see widespread chaos emanating from a decision by the judge to exercise discretion in this manner; the same perception should be applied to the jury that nullifies. This would, however, necessitate a more mature understanding of the juror than the schoolhouse model allows.

The trial of John Peter Zenger in 1735 offers an opportunity to consider the value of treating jurors as radically enfranchised citizens capable of resisting the will of the state when necessary.[10] Zenger, publisher of the *New-York Weekly Journal*, was charged with seditious libel for criticizing the royal governor of the colony. While the judge was clearly in favor of the governor and of the state's case against the publisher, Zenger's defense was argued by the former attorney general of Pennsylvania, Andrew Hamilton, who presented an argument about truth as a defense against libel. He directed this argument to the jury, tacitly acknowledging that he was asking them to make a decision without precedent in colonial case law. The jury found Zenger not guilty, accepting Hamilton's argument and changing the nature of future prosecution for libel. The action of the jury represented a radically enfranchised response because the jurors did not take the established law and its historical application as the essence of justice. Grounded in their knowledge of the conditions of political life, they were persuaded by a conception of the free press and the privilege to hear truths about the political actions of the sovereign, however unsavory or negative they may be. While this example shows the jury taking a position directly critical of the power of the sovereign, other types of actions salient in this model of political maturity include those critical of enforcement or policing.

In some ways, the larger argument about juries as spaces where radical enfranchisement can occur, and may even require breaking with the established norms of what juries are supposed to do, can be seen as a critique of proceduralism—the idea that legitimacy is determined by whether the proper steps were followed rather than a substantive assessment of the final decision—that often characterizes the American criminal justice system. A strict emphasis on proceduralism could be partially to blame, as James Q. Whitman says, for the harsh standards of punishment in this country, including rates of incarceration, imprisonment for property crimes, and the continued use of the death penalty.[11] An alternative to proceduralism is a greater emphasis on substantive justice and the awareness that the judgment required for decisions about punishment is always a careful triangulation of multiple considerations and a prioritizing of certain values over others, even if all are central to democracy.[12] Proceduralism as an ideal was a means to protect against vagaries and prejudices of an arbitrary system and to ensure the protection of defendant rights against the excesses of the state. Yet once a procedure has become compromised in its application or when it contributes to the perpetuation of an undemocratic status quo, the possibility of an action that goes against established procedure may be desirable. Such an outlook has affinities with theories of the nonideal—specifically the sense that, in nonideal circumstances, extraordinary acts are needed to demonstrate a commitment to certain ideals such that the procedures can be brought into alignment with these ideals. A less flawed reality would have fewer extraordinary acts. Yet it is also true that even with well-functioning procedures, there may be legitimate reasons for unusual interventions by the jury.

Tocqueville strikes a careful tone when he distinguishes the republican value of self-legislation within juries from the anarchy of revolt. Jurors without the strict guidance of the law and the officers of the court, he implies, may take their power too far and will invite instability in precisely the institution that should be most governed by procedure. The argument here for the cultivation of political maturity is an argument against both revolution and strict proceduralism. Yet the way in which Tocqueville describes and understands revolution makes it difficult for him to understand how more isolated and contained moments of dissent, especially those that challenge the way a law is applied, could be constructive. A political theory that includes exceptional moments of jury decision-making is, in fact, a blind spot that is evident in Tocqueville's perception of revolution. I follow Sheldon Wolin when he writes, "The extreme abstractness, which he attributes to revolutionary theory—to its ideas of natural right, the sovereignty of the people, the equality of all, and the absolute rejection of all traditional institutions and beliefs—and his refusal to discriminate among competing theories, allows Tocqueville to compact them into a form of myth rather than deal with them as arguments."[13] When any challenge to conventional authority is seen as part of the myth of redemptive revolution, it can never be justified, moderated, or contextualized. The delicate balance of local and federal power, lay and expert, mass and elite, has been damaged. Democracy has already, in Tocqueville's mind, conceded so much to the egoistic needs of the people in allowing them to be seen as estimable even in their mediocrity, that to suggest that there are moments (exceptional, to be sure) when the jury should be skeptical of the legitimacy of the law offers far too much latitude to laypeople. Such latitude is, however, consistent with an understanding of the juror as a radically enfranchised actor who develops skills through jury service that may be used to promote an interpretation of the law that is counter to conventional applications.

Tocqueville's reputation as a great advocate for juries is accurate, but only to a certain degree, and I am influenced by Albert Dzur's analysis of the ways that an uncritical acceptance of Tocqueville's appreciation of the jury obscures how it might undermine other desirable functions of the jury.[14] He posits that the jury is fundamentally a check on elite and professional power. It is not that jury members are bestowed a magistracy that comes from proximity to the aristocratic classes of judges and lawyers, but rather, Dzur suggests, the distinctive role they play as nonprofessionals in an institution dominated by professionals. Dzur writes, "What is useful in Tocqueville's account of the jury as a school can be deployed in contemporary debates only if we take care to notice how the jury is also not a school but a site that gathers, focuses and uses the already existing juridical capabilities of lay people."[15]

Unexpectedly, it is Thomas Hobbes who provides a persuasive approach to the power of juries, one that is consistent with a productively agonistic understanding of legal life. Observing the unchecked power of the Star Chamber and the tendency of the judiciary to become too powerful, Hobbes writes,

> In like manner, in the ordinary trials of Right, Twelve men of the common People, are the Judges, and give Sentence, not only of the Fact, but of the Right; and pronounce simply for the Complaynant, or for the Defendant; that is to say, are Judges not only of the Fact, but also of the Right: and in a question of crime, not only determine whether done, or not done; but also whether it be Murder, Homicide, Felony, Assault, and the like, which are determinations of Law: but because they are not supposed to know the Law of themselves, there is one that hath Authority to enforme them of it, in the particular case they are to Judge of.[16]

As "Judges . . . of Right" in addition to "Fact," Hobbes places the power of judgment in the jury and and renounces the tradition of punishing juries who reach a verdict contra the desire of the judge. Hobbes is navigating a path between imagining the community conscience embodied in the jury (and its affinity with the natural law tradition) and justice grounded in positive law and the aspiration to formality and consistency that the rule of law is said to bring. Hobbes sees value neither in appealing to a higher law (as in natural law) nor in deferring to the officers of the legal code (positive law), but rather takes a skeptical position in relation to both. It is critical for the jury to have ultimate discretionary power to judge the aptness of a guilty verdict without recourse to an outside source of authority, as convenient as it might be to treat such a source as sacrosanct. As Richard Tuck writes, "The jurors should think of themselves not merely as equally the representative of the sovereign as the judge, but as superior to the judge: they were the real representatives, and the judge was merely an adviser. Given that (as Hobbes constantly reminded his readers) the real power over the laws was the power of interpretation, the fact that the jurors could not be prevented from taking up any view they chose about the meaning of the laws gave them enormous authority, which Hobbes seems to have gone out of his way to welcome."[17]

Tuck places the emphasis on the right of the jury to interpretation, and thus draws a link to the role of the Leviathan itself, which has the power to assign definitions to words. The factual truth of the crime is only one contributing factor to the truth of the verdict; the decision to declare a defendant not guilty may be tethered to other truths and the language chosen to represent them. The force of Hobbes's defense of the jury is unexpected because of the way it suggests that the people, seemingly excluded from political power in the Hobbesian state, have a critical role to play in the legal system. The motivation becomes more apparent when thinking about juries as making a distinction between citizen and criminal that has implications for the legitimacy of violence promulgated by the state, arguably Hobbes's ultimate concern. Radical enfranchisement can also be seen as consistent with Hobbes's protest that the type of adjudication open to the House of Lords, with all the reasonableness and generosity that elite comradery might entail, should be available to all who are charged with a crime. To be judged by a jury of one's peers, where each person has one vote, is one of the best forms of decision-making to prevent the abuse of power.

In the spirit of a Hobbesian derogation of power to the jury and contra Tocqueville's schoolhouse model, Dzur looks to the analysis of German-American political scientist Francis Lieber (1798–1872), who held juries to be "ambivalent—not automatically trusting but careful about the knowledge and guidance of courthouse regulars."[18] Thus, the relationship between juries and the court and its officers, while symbiotic by all accounts, takes on a more agonistic valence in Lieber's writing. While Tocqueville's support for the jury's deference to professional knowledge diverges from how he understands the town hall meeting, for example, Dzur suggests that a more ambivalent approach to the professionalism of the court is an aspect worth highlighting in the contemporary context. The fact of conflict between the jury and others is not a threat to the legal system but a sign that it is, in fact, bringing voices that are often excluded into the legal and political process in a meaningful way.

Lieber's position is consistent with the role of the jury within the common law tradition through the American revolutionary period. From the precedent set in the case of William Penn (known as Bushel's case after the jury foreman who brought suit), the jury as the ultimate arbiter of the law was cemented and extended to include a consistent strong hand in deciding on the law, not just on the facts of the case.[19] In the medieval common law framework, the strengths of the jury—its proximity to the agents involved in the case, knowledge of social mores, and antielite sensibilities—were assets in determining how the law should be enforced, not merely to assess whether the facts were consistent with a standard for evidence. The anti-Federalists would carry this mantle through the ratification period but, as the Federalist cause of centralized and consistently applied legal power took hold, the value of the jury as a robust local institution gradually declined. It was not just the check on state power that declined as jury power receded; there was a corresponding loss in thinking about jurors as harboring an epistemological and moral position distinct from other legal actors. Shannon Stimson recalls this trajectory when she writes, "It appears that for an increasing number of newly independent Americans, the demands of achieving some degree of legal uniformity in the aftermath of the Revolution, not only within the newly legitimated 'states' but especially within the nation at large, required a curtailment of the jury's significant lawfinding powers. In particular, historians have suggested that jural powers were curtailed for largely economic reasons, because the 'certainty and predictability of substantive rules that a commercial economy required would be to little avail if juries remained free to reject those rules or to apply them inconsistently.' "[20]

The economic impact of jury decisions, most notably in civil cases but also in criminal cases, continues to play a large role in the skepticism surrounding arguments for a heightened awareness of jury power. In determining who should be punished and, in certain cases, for how long and in what way, a guilty verdict is the most dramatic decision a citizen can make. Tocqueville goes so far as to call a juror the "master of society," but could this be understood in a somewhat ironic way, given his fears about the maintenance of social order that are woven through his reflections on democracy? Can juries deflect accountability from the true "master[s] of society"—that elite group that serves as representatives and judges? If so, can we think about jurors as being duped by this responsibility, that is, are they led to believe that they are the deciders, when in fact the outcome has been orchestrated from the start? This is perhaps one of the most cynical, though not uncommon, takes on the adversarial system—the performance of the trial is precisely that, a performance that obscures as much as it reveals where performers (officers of the court) can use sleight of hand to suggest agency in one part of the courtroom when in fact much greater power exists in another. Lawyers cannot rig the jury box, but they can calibrate their efforts in a trial to facilitate one outcome or another. Tocqueville describes this starkly when talking about a civil jury: "The jurors pronounce the ruling that the judge has rendered. To his ruling, they lend the authority of the society that they represent, and he, that of the reason and of the law."[21] The jury thus serves to legitimate the decision that the judge, with his education, experience, and likely history of privilege has decided; again, the republican aspects of the jury lauded by Tocqueville are worthwhile only when carefully bounded.

Giving the jury a central role in the determination of whether the state will use punishment makes it complicit in the infliction of physical suffering. Robert Cover has argued that what distinguishes legal interpretation from other types of language is its relationship to legitimate violence.[22] Judges sit in uneasy relation to this reality, at times trying to distance themselves from it—and what better way to do this than by distributing the tasks necessary for such an act? In Cover's words, "Because legal interpretation is as a practice incomplete without violence—because it depends upon the social practice of violence for its efficacy—it must be related in a strong way to the cues that operate to bypass or *suppress the psycho-social mechanisms that usually inhibit people's actions* causing pain and death."[23] The jury, it can be argued, is one of the most effective psychosocial mechanisms to make decisions that enact violence for which individuals, judges or not, may have difficulty taking responsibility. The framework of a group of laypeople with no further role in the criminal justice system provides the best form of a legitimate institution that is difficult to scrutinize after the fact. Tocqueville himself understood the value of having the most distressing part of the judicial process derogated to the people in the context of a democracy rather than to the elite officials of the court. Thus, the emphasis on the jury's burden in punishment plays a complex role within the balance of power between nonelite laypeople and the expert class of lawyers, judges, and elites. While they have genuine power, they also act as a buffer that protects elite officials from censure. Highlighting their status as radically enfranchised citizens may further allow criticism to be deflected from those responsible for perpetuating the injustices of the status quo, among other things. Yet, it is my hope that the further galvanization of jurors to act based on the knowledge and experiences that they bring to the courtroom, even when it is contrary to the expressed position of law enforcement, is in the service of greater uptake on the most vexing problems of the criminal justice system and a type of intellectual discipline that will also be useful for political life.

On Women

Although Tocqueville's perception of women in *Democracy in America* represents a set of observations of social mores, rather than legal institutions, there are similarities in the promise of political maturity he saw in women and what he saw in jurors. By discussing the two together, the hope is that juror maturity, a concept previously hard to imagine, will benefit from the transformed perceptions of women's maturity, albeit vexed, in the contemporary era. In his time, Tocqueville found much to celebrate in the conditions of American women, particularly in their education, sense of independence, and competence in understanding complex social realities. In contrast to young European women of similar social status, American girls were not sheltered from the reality of the public world and were given the confidence and intellectual training to opine on such conditions, at least during adolescence. He writes:

> Long before the young American woman has attained the age of puberty, one begins to free her little by little from maternal tutelage; before she has entirely left childhood she already thinks for herself, speaks freely, and acts alone; the great picture of the world is constantly exposed before her; far from seeking to conceal the view of it from her, they uncover more and more of it to her regard every day and teach her to consider it with a firm and tranquil eye. Thus the vices and perils that society presents are not slow to be revealed to her; she sees them clearly, judges them without illusion, and faces them without fear; for she is full of confidence in her strength, and her confidence seems to be shared by all those who surround her.[24]

Tocqueville appears taken with the remarkably high level of autonomy and decision-making capacity in young American women and attributes this, in part, to the challenges of democracy—the "tyrannical passion of the human heart" and the contested shores of public opinion. Women are given an education in civic virtue, and the tool of reason, rather than the script of religion, is the countervailing force to the liberty and licentiousness that are more prominent in democracy than in aristocratic regimes. It is notable that Tocqueville does not temper his discussion of young women with comparisons to their brothers—on whom they seem to neither depend for the protection of their virtue nor defer to in matters of cognitive capacity. Young women are ensconced in the protection and didacticism of the family, one that is headed by a man, but the independence Tocqueville notices in girls is not perpetually bound to a male figure. Remarkably, American girls are primed to conduct themselves in a world where authority is diffuse and may exist in conflicting configurations.

If Tocqueville appears to be empirically driven in his thinking about the particular sociological qualities of the experiences of American girls and women, the one framing normative concept he brings to these observations is the idea that "women make mores," and that the task for adult women is to cultivate these mores in the private, domestic sphere. The moment of marriage marks a sharp contrast from the independence nurtured in girl-hood. Though not without its value and even necessity in Tocqueville's ac-count, "the independence of woman is irretrievably lost within the bonds of marriage."[25] Marriage, a relationship undertaken by mature women, be-comes a space in which to cultivate distinct religious and secular ideals, including those of deference, self-abnegation, and frugality. Religious vir-tues now become more important than ethical judgments as the foil for the individualism and commercialism of the public sphere.

The equality of conditions that fostered the spirit of gumption in their youth also gave women the semblance of choice when it came to choosing a husband (the ideology of antimiscegenation and class prejudice notwith-standing), in contrast to the arranged marriages with which Tocqueville was familiar. Yet after the act of making the marital choice, their worldly knowl-edge and gumption were not particularly useful. He writes, "Almost all men in democracies follow a political career or exercise a profession, and, on the other hand, the mediocrity of fortunes obliges a woman to confine herself inside her dwelling every day in order to preside herself very closely over the details of domestic administration."[26] While the responsibilities for hus-bands and wives are defined and distinct, such conditions allow for the process of true affection, Tocqueville postures, between men and women because of their complementarity in the context of love and respect. Schol-ars have argued that while the idea of two spheres, public and private, with the former superior to the latter, is taken as immutable, Tocqueville does not attribute it to the differences of the body.[27] De-emphasizing the biologically determinative aspects of the division of labor allows Tocqueville to high-light the political and moral value of such an arrangement.

Moreover, Tocqueville finds the strictness of such an arrangement to be voluntarily, even enthusiastically, supported by the women themselves. They are far too capable to be fooled into submission, although Tocqueville gestures toward his own socioeconomic myopia when he says, in reference to the harmonious division of labor, "That is at least the sentiment that the most virtuous women express: the others are silent."[28] Still deference to the authority of one's husband, coupled with a soft prohibition on public life, results in a case of the arrested development of American women. It is unfortunate because adult women seem to be particularly well poised to engage with the mores of society because of their own position vis-à-vis tradition. Again, Tocqueville's historical determinism makes it difficult to know whether he genuinely did not notice opportunities for greater female involvement in democratic life or the desire for it by women themselves (in part a problem with how he scheduled his trip), or whether he saw domestic confinement as a necessary constraint on the intellectual and political capabilities of women.

Were there to be the assumption of radical enfranchisement, women would be particularly competent in deciding punishment given Tocqueville's description. Their civic and moral education as young adults, marked, as he says, by an awareness of the realities of social problems without the paralysis of fear, would be a fitting precursor to the judgments necessary for punishment. Similarly, given the role of women in cultivating and perpetuating social mores apart from individualism and consumerism, they would also be capable of determining how punishments might contribute to the furthering of social ends, especially in the deterrent and rehabilitative functions of punishment. Again, both jurors and women have the potential to do the difficult and important work of determining punishment, but Tocqueville hobbles their abilities to do so.

Feminist scholarship has taken up the question of the significance of such a stark contrast in what Tocqueville valued in the life trajectories of youthful versus mature American women. A revival of interest in Tocqueville in the 1980s combined with greater attention to the gendered dimensions of the work led to more generous readings. Notably, Delba Winthrop suggested that Tocqueville's comfort with the confined role of women came from his understanding about the false promises of democracy and commercial life. Women's distance from the public world means that they are better off, not worse, because they are less compromised in their marketized daily exchanges and less prone to be driven by the narcissism democracy dares its practitioners to display. She writes, "Informed resignation to democracy's defects is as much as a woman or a man can reasonably hope to accomplish in (and for) democracy. . . . To raise our collective consciousness, flout conventions and overturn or amend our laws" will only exacerbate the worst aspects of democratic life.[29] Winthrop is thus a sympathetic reader of Tocqueville's aristocratic yearnings—for her, it is best to keep democracy in check, even if it is done through mechanisms that rely on the confinement of human potential. Yet her reading supports the larger argument in that the radical enfranchisement of women—that is, the chance to flout conventions and overturn laws—is the process by which democracy evolves. If there is an equilibrium where aristocratic fears are kept in check, might there be another where some of the causes for revolution (inequality, *ressentiment*, etc.) are mitigated by greater political participation?

Laura Janara's work sees Tocqueville's defense of the boundary between the independent girl and the subservient woman as tied to his subconscious desires to both preserve and obscure the hierarchical arrangements that provide stability within aristocratic regimes. The playful esteem in which Tocqueville seems to hold American women belies deeper fears about what might emerge if they were to be seen as mature democratic citizens. She writes, "Even as this adult female soothes democracy's post-aristocratic anxieties, she continually pricks them. In relegating women to the household in order to install a new certainty in society, U.S. democracy staves off some of the tumult. But these women's deep influence—over mores and morality, bodies and erotic desire—undoubtedly triggers the opposing fear that, through them somehow, authority-from-above will reincarnate to dissolve men's newfound autonomy."[30] Such a psychoanalytic reading suggests that the arrested development of women as full political subjects may be the source of a double bind for male political subjects who feel anxious even when they are at their best, that is, when they are trying to achieve a balance between democratic procedures and an aristocratic tilt toward tradition and excellence. The double bind is as follows: on the one hand, the achievement of the full emancipation of women in a way that builds on the education and autonomy that have developed in democratic life would destabilize the privilege of masculinity that democracy offers alongside its rhetoric of equality. On the other hand, the continued suppression of female competency contributes to greater anxieties about the potential for instability in a democracy and the resentment that comes from unfulfilled promises. Tocqueville may deny that such anxiety is operational for men within democracy, but his blithe observations about the gap between the potential of female education and autonomy and their use evinces another historical trajectory that should be possible.

For Tocqueville to see jurors and women as radically enfranchised, he must afford them the opportunity to diverge from those who were instrumental in their education in order to enact a belief about the proper application of justice. For jurors, this would be divergence from the officers of the court, including the judge and attorneys, and for women, it would be the teachers and family elders of their childhood. The possibility of a legitimate difference in viewpoints from one's husband, although he is not necessarily tasked with female education, also represents a type of enfranchisement for women as it takes them to have insight and value in decisions beyond the private sphere. Radical enfranchisement in the case of jurors does not refer to the potential to break the procedures of the court per se, but, when the conditions necessitate it, for the jury to nullify the law in a particular case or to be part of a minority that causes a hung jury. While both outcomes are technically acceptable, judges and lawyers frown upon them. For jurors to act in a radically enfranchised way does not mean that they can never be criticized for their actions—they will make mistakes or errors in judgment (just like prosecutors and judges) and this will cause public debate, but the starting assumption is that jury decisions in exceptional moments should be treated with greater attention and as a symptom of a functioning democracy.

The Ills of Democracy

Thus far I have showed that Tocqueville fails to see the possibility and necessity of the radical enfranchisement of jurors and women despite his own observations and assessments that both groups could meet such a standard. His own biases, psychological and theoretical, along with a sociological method that affirms the immanent as the normative prevents him from seeing the opportunities of radical enfranchisement for the two major ills of democracy that vex him: the tyranny of the majority and soft despotism. On the power of the majority to enact its will, he writes, "The majority in the United States therefore has an immense power in fact, and a power in opinion almost as great; and once it has formed a question, there are so to speak no obstacles that can, I shall not say stop, but even delay its advance, and allow it the time to hear the complaints of those it crushes as it passes."[31] The protection of individual rights enshrined within the Bill of Rights acts as a dam to the tides of majority desires, but the jury also tempers the tyranny of the majority through determining how and when the law should be applied. Tocqueville addresses this function directly, but for reasons described above does not highlight the even greater potential of the jury to resist majoritarian goals by enacting one-off outcomes that challenge the necessary proceduralism of democracy for the purposes of substantive justice.

The problem of soft despotism occurs when a political system is so governed by complex and tedious rules that acquiescence and passivity become conscious political choices for citizens who are politically aware. Soft despotism, a danger to democracy in Tocqueville's view, exists in productive tension with jury service. On the one hand, skeptics of juries (along with those who bemoan being served a summons for jury duty) would highlight the aspects of jury service that feel like tedious procedure. From the artifice of the trial to rules against casual discussion among jurors or note taking, many aspects of the legal system are decidedly opaque and difficult for outsiders to navigate. The prosecution in a criminal case, one might argue, exercises its own type of soft despotism within the criminal justice system because of its knowledge of the legal code and the comradery that often develops between police officer, prosecutor, and officers of the court.

Compared with despotism conventionally understood, soft despotism engenders the same enfeebled will and impoverished sense of political possibility but does so without resentment against the oppressive sovereign. On the other hand, jury service and the empowerment of jurors could be an antidote to soft despotism. Jury service is, for many groups who have been traditionally excluded from political power because of race, class, gender, or other reasons, a type of Trojan horse that passes through the traditional fortifications of soft despotism. Jurors are given final decision-making power and the chance to interpret the law in a way that reflects their understanding of justice. Rather than the acquiescence that comes with soft despotism, jury service is active and carries an impact different from other types of civic service. Giving jurors further legitimacy to act on the epistemological and moral perspective they bring to the courtroom and refine through deliberation is a way to counter the pervasiveness of soft despotism.

In the cases of the jury and women, radical enfranchisement is a process that includes education, internal reflection, and deliberation, and it should find expression within the legal and political system, particularly through the opportunity to make decisions that have direct impact. Such power would come with the responsibility to understand the limitations of both tradition and revolution. Radical enfranchisement is thus a position between complicity and reckless agitation. Jurors arrive at such a position through the status that is granted to their service, their education in legal procedure during and after the trial, the leadership of judges and lawyers, jurors' deliberations with each other, and the filtering of life experiences in light of the law that occurs when one is called to make a judgment. In the vast majority of cases, the decision of the jury will follow the guidelines set forth by the judge and by case history, but there will also be extraordinary circumstances that require an activation of their distinctive perspective. My argument for thinking about jurors as radically enfranchised subjects capable of deciding between multiple values and conceptions of justice and capable of going against the wishes of the officers of the court, in the case of a hung jury for example, is indebted to Tocqueville and all the work his writings have inspired about juries and democratic life. Yet, situating his enthusiasm for juries alongside his hesitations, especially as revealed in his examination of women, shows how there is a need for a projury position that cannot be Tocquevillian in spirit, because it requires a pivot to the left— with increased prominence for juries as a way to insert *more* democracy as the remedy for a *poisoned* democracy—when Tocqueville pivots to the right with his focus on the benefits of aristocratic exposure.

TWO

Mistaken for Consensus:
Hung Juries, the Allen Charge, and
the End of Jury Deliberation

Each jury is a little Parliament. The jury sense is the parliamentary sense. I cannot
see the one dying and the other surviving. The first object of any tyrant in Whitehall
would be to make the Parliament utterly subservient to his will; and the next to
overthrow or diminish trial by jury, for no tyrant could afford to have a subject's
freedom in the hands of twelve of his countrymen.

—Lord Devlin, *Trial by Jury*

The declaration of a hung jury is one of the most dramatic moments in
the legal process. All of the resources and efforts invested in a trial can be
perceived to have been for naught when a jury expected to reach a unanimous verdict (either guilty or not guilty) fails to do so. For the defendant,
a hung jury may be celebrated as a brief reprieve—there will be another
trial or pressure to plea bargain from the state, but it is significant that a
jury of one's peers did not find the evidence adequately convincing. For
the prosecution, the hung jury is likely felt as a waste of time and money.
The judge often has a more ambivalent perspective; she may understand
why the jury failed to reach a consensus, but is still disappointed with the
outcome of a mistrial (almost always cause for greater official scrutiny of the
decisions of the judge). This chapter examines when the hung jury should
be understood as a mistake, that is, an outcome that reveals a breakdown in
the procedures of the trial or undermines the tenets of the adversarial justice
system. The hung jury is a sanctioned option within US law, so should not
be seen as an aberration, but the mixed reactions to it suggest room for interpretation about what it reveals about the jury process and the obstacles to
consensus.

An orientation of radical enfranchisement enriches an understanding of the hung jury because it draws attention to the validity of dissensus on the two most important questions for the jury: the weight of the evidence and the appropriateness of punishment. Disagreement surrounding both may be the cause of a hung jury, but the deliberative process scaffolded by the trial is still critical for legitimacy and includes the commitment of the radically enfranchised juror to weigh aspects of judgment that one might not in one's personal life (such as the presumption of innocence, discussed elsewhere) as well as the dangers of prejudicial logic. Ignoring these responsibilities cannot be the foundation for a hung jury, but, as this chapter suggests, radical enfranchisement can make jurors better attuned to worldview differences among themselves. It can support the knowledge that dissensus after rigorous deliberation can be consistent with the highest ideals of the trial.

The hung jury is also a highly significant outcome for the judge because it results in a mistrial. To prevent such an outcome, a judge may issue a version of the Allen Charge, a second set of instructions to a jury that appears to be struggling to reach unanimity. The judge may address topics such as the expense of the trial, the value of the randomness of the jury selection process, and the expectations of reasonable doubt in order to motivate the jury to reach a verdict. The Allen Charge is one of the more controversial aspects of jury procedure, alternately seen as helpful or coercive depending on the context, and its illegality in twenty-three states attests to this status. An investigation into the Allen Charge sharpens the question and offers insights, via contrast, into what a productively adversarial relationship between judge and a radically enfranchised jury might look like.

The conceptual armature of Jürgen Habermas's work on discourse ethics is relevant to the question of hung juries because of the ways in which jury procedure within the US legal system manifests some of Habermas's central philosophical ideals, but has not been the object of his attention. Written in a more abstract register, Habermas's defense of discourse ethics is meant to generate a means for testing the legitimacy of norms, but his work also gives insight into the conditions that would be desirable for decisions as immediate and pragmatic as jury verdicts. Using his formulations of the Ideal Speech Situation and of the lifeworld as conceptual touchstones allows for an interpretation of the legitimate hung jury as a highly significant outcome and one that can be seen as the opposite of a mistake. Through this lens, the Allen Charge also comes into focus as a misguided attempt to offset a potentially erroneous outcome with a coercive intervention.

The Allen Charge

Led by Chief Justice Fuller, a unanimous decision of the Supreme Court in 1896 decided that the judge's instructions to the jury nearing a deadlock, what would come to be known as the Allen Charge, were not improper. The fact that the presiding judge spoke about the purpose of the trial, the resources involved, the integrity of the jurors, and the responsibility of minority jurors to reconsider their position were found to be acceptable and even beneficial to the jury deliberation process. The model charge from the Fifth Circuit that was approved by the court reads:

Members of the Jury:

I'm going to ask that you continue your deliberations in an effort to reach agreement upon a verdict and dispose of this case; and I have a few additional comments I would like for you to consider as you do so. This is an important case. The trial has been expensive in time, effort, money and emotional strain to both the defense and the prosecution. If you should fail to agree upon a verdict, the case will be left open and may have to be tried again. Obviously, another trial would only serve to increase the cost to both sides, and there is no reason to believe that the case can be tried again by either side any better or more exhaustively than it has been tried before you. Any future jury must be selected in the same manner and from the same source as you were chosen, and there is no reason to believe that the case could ever be submitted to twelve men and women more conscientious, more impartial, or more competent to decide it, or that more or clearer evidence could be produced. If a substantial majority of your number are in favor of a conviction, those of you who disagree should reconsider whether your doubt is a reasonable one since it appears to make no effective impression upon the minds of the others. On the other hand, if a majority or even a lesser number of you are in favor of an acquittal, the rest of you should ask yourselves again, and most thoughtfully, whether you should accept the weight and sufficiency of evidence which fails to convince your fellow jurors beyond a reasonable doubt. Remember at all times that no juror is expected to give up an honest belief he or she may have as to the weight or effect of the evidence; but, after full deliberation and consideration of the evidence in the case, it is your duty to agree upon a verdict if you can do so. You must also remember that if the evidence in the case fails to establish guilt beyond a reasonable doubt the Defendant should have your unanimous verdict of Not Guilty. You may be as leisurely in your deliberations as the occasion may require and should take all the time which you may feel is necessary.

The tone of the charge is intriguing and I am drawn to the controversy because of the tension between the judicious and measured language of the charge that appears to treat those in favor and not in favor of a conviction with equanimity, and the palpable feeling that the jury is being scolded for the uncooperative actions of a few. In the contemporary legal landscape, states that allow intervention by the judge in this manner offer charges similar in tone and content. While judges are not expected to read verbatim from the model charge, certain points are to be observed, in part to defend against appellate reversal; they include asking both majority and minority jurors to listen to the opposing side's argument and ensuring that jurors know that they are not expected to "give up an honest belief."[1] Case law since the time of the Allen decision has codified some of the most controversial aspects of the charge, also known as the "dynamite charge," and it has revealed an oft-repeated set of arguments that dissenting judges use to question its validity.

Representative of their concerns, the Coleman dissent in *Thaggard v. US* (1965) posits the Allen Charge as a "plea from the bench for a verdict" and is an elegant appeal to interpret the Sixth Amendment right to an impartial jury to mean a jury that is free from the interference of a judge clearly invested in a *unanimous* verdict.[2] From Coleman's perspective, even with the acknowledgment of the responsibilities of the majority and minority jurors, the charge still creates a disproportionate demand on dissenting voters who believe they are in violation of the judge's wishes for unanimity. He is particularly aggrieved with the language used by the lower-court judge who told the jury in the course of extrapolating on the Allen Charge that the "case must at some time be decided." Coleman suggested that such language effaces the option of a hung jury from the set of legitimate outcomes, even though it is a protected one that is in the spirit of an adversarial system of justice that presumes the innocence of the defendant. The fact that there is a heavy burden of proof on the state for a conviction should not lead to frustration expressed by the judge and then ameliorated by the jury. Coleman's concerns capture the legal establishment's reasons for withholding support for the Allen Charge, despite its claims to efficiency and fairness.[3] The argument elaborated in the rest of the chapter dovetails with these concerns, yet it approaches the question of the Allen Charge from the perspective of the expectations of deliberative democracy and the conceptual validity of the hung jury.[4]

Highlighting the hung jury as a legitimate outcome, one that captures important worldview differences about what justice would require in the given situation, underscores the notion of justice to which radical enfranchisement aspires. A criminal trial activates the judgment of citizens in order to decide the facts of the case, the material basis for the charge, and the normative question as to whether or not punishment is desirable, as all are essential for justice. The hung jury, based on principled disagreement, is a limiting case that makes real the intellectual and ethical alchemy desirable in all verdicts.

My interpretation of the jury process has many affinities with Robert Burns's understanding of the trial as an idiosyncratic institution that gives rise to its own particular (and admirable) form of judgment, one that depends on the agonistic struggle of a variety of norms and linguistic practices.[5] The trial is an insular world, not appropriate for translation into other social or political models, and attempts to do so rely on the specious isolation of desirable forms of reasoning. The jury, in his assessment, must be able to render a decision free of monitoring and quality control by the judge because of the complicated nature of the decision. It is not the contingency of the decision process, the relationship between particulars, or the universalism of the law (though that is part of it) that mark the distinctiveness of the jury's responsibility, Burns argues, but the multilayered way in which jurors decide about narrative coherence, social norms, and legal ideals in a way that exceeds the conventions of deductive reasoning.

An investigation into the "mistake" of a hung jury raises a critical question about the relationship between the judge and jury: should the judge be understood as the "boss" of the jury, insuring that the jurors do their jobs properly? On the one hand, it is the responsibility of the judge to impart her highly specialized knowledge about trial procedure to the jury such that there are not grounds for a mistrial. There will be times when the proper procedure is counter to both the will and instinct of the jury (such as the desire to talk about the trial with family members or on social media) and they must be instructed that their willingness to follow procedure is not a matter of discretion. The judge is thus a manager with the power to punish and sanction when expectations are not met. On the other hand, the roles of judge and jury change once the jury instructions are given. At this point, the judge is less like a boss than an umpire, one who does not have say in the strategy of the game but upholds a minimum standard of integrity. While the judge may still admonish jurors for violating court procedure, deliberation occurs in a closed room. The fact that the jury has the ultimate authority to decide within the adversarial system is interpreted to mean that the jury should not be monitored, coerced, led, or criticized by the judge or counsel as it is making its decision. The jury has a right to ask the judge questions about its task, but the jurors are no longer under her watchful eye. They are expected to take their responsibility seriously, but the judge cannot tell them that their decision is wrong (as Bushel's case famously established in 1670).[6] The argument below will suggest that the Allen Charge should be seen as an inappropriate switch to the boss model of judicial authority. The jury has been entrusted with a task and it is consistent with the other procedures of jury deliberation to let the jury manifest this trust by giving it the freedom to conduct deliberations in the best way that it can. The jury that is unable to reach consensus should not be treated as if it has strayed from its responsibility and needs the supervision of a boss. Yet what if the jury deliberates for only two minutes and returns a guilty verdict? What should the judge do then? It seems plausible to say that in two minutes there would be barely enough time to poll the jury members, let alone "deliberate" about the evidence. Still, I follow Burns in his interpretation of the complex mandate of the jury, one that challenges the received view of the primacy of proceduralism in regards to the letter of the law. The jury must navigate between multiple linguistic and cognitive practices and must be given the latitude by the judge to do it in the best manner the jurors see fit. The Allen Charge interrupts the insular world of the jury and suggests that sheer willpower or improved deductive reasoning will allow the majority to see the viewpoint of the minority or vice versa. Such an assumption about the jury's deliberation flattens the process at precisely the moment when the conditions for deliberation must be expansive and beyond inherited formulas.[7]

On the Philosophy of Jürgen Habermas

With his attention to conditions that could foster communicative rationality, Jürgen Habermas provides a path out of the impasse of cynicism and political impossibility to which critical theory has arguably succumbed. Instead of a perspective that maintains that the political and moral spheres have been irretrievably marred by ideology and the corrosive effects of both liberalism and capitalism, his conception of communicative rationality suggests a redirection of the Enlightenment project away from instrumental rationality and toward ends that are inclusive and mutually beneficial. The ability of individuals to understand each other through everyday language, even if they begin from disparate premises, allows for the possibility of relationships that are not based solely on domination and exploitation.[8] Such communicative rationality also allows for the generation of new moral norms that garner their legitimacy from a much more inclusive process than previously theorized. The legitimacy of moral and political norms should, in his framework, thus be tied to the structural and linguistic conditions of participation in their creation, rather than to tradition and an imagined premise of consent based on reason.[9]

The heuristic of the Ideal Speech Situation is Habermas's potent vision of the conditions necessary to have the kind of communicative exchange in which intersubjective recognition is possible and which is capable of generating legitimate norms. It is important to note that Habermas never expected the Ideal Speech Situation to be a blueprint for existing political institutions nor to serve, as did Rousseau's general will, as an empirical fantasy. Habermas is adamantly not calling for direct democracy in a new era and does not want to make the mistake that he claims Rousseau to have made, that is to have confused his new model of legitimacy with a new model for political engagement.[10] It is thus the *conceptual* preconditions for legitimacy that are of the utmost concern. In placing these conditions in conversation with the jury deliberation process, I am not emphasizing procedural reforms that would make them more in line with the Ideal Speech Situation, yet, the concerns Habermas raises about the conditions for deliberation and the opportunities for the distortion of such a process can be brought to bear on thinking about the hung jury.

The Ideal Speech Situation is premised on two conditions: The first condition (U) is grounded in the assumption of universalization, that is, the assumption that for a norm to be valid, *each* individual would be able to accept it without coercion through the process of a reasonable discourse about its effects and consequences.[11] A norm becomes universalized and universalizable through the fact that its consequences are acceptable to every person and that this acceptance is reached without the coercion that can be the result of vastly unequal positions of power. The fact that each person holds the right to accept independently is central to the moral force of the outcome. The demand for unanimity, with all the challenges it implies, is the proper condition for determining the validity of norms within a system of thought that places intersubjective communication at the core of its political and moral project.

In many other fora, the need for closure is so urgent that majority rule is thought to be the most pragmatic expectation for arriving at a decision. There are many political or administrative issues on which reasonable people disagree and, given this reality, the argument goes, the will of the majority (usually a compromise in itself) must suffice to render a decision and thus make it possible for a governing body to move on to other issues or take action. However, within Habermas's framework for the legitimation of *moral* norms, the condition that all those who are affected must agree is not a secondary concern. Rather, it is meant to be the site of contestation and should not be obscured by strategic concerns or a type of realist pessimism that suggests that majority agreement is the best outcome one can hope for. It is not correct to equate Habermas's condition of unanimity for the legitimacy of a moral norm with an argument for the strict standard of unanimity in juries. Yet, there are still affinities—there are issues, both for Habermas and in the case of juries, that are too important to risk the kind of intellectual exclusion of unpopular positions that majority rule allows. It is important to note that revisability is always in the array of possibilities regarding the legitimation of norms. Forced closure could never be compatible with the normative requirements of the Ideal Speech Situation; the real and the ideal should not be collapsed. If consensus only appears asymptotically in reference to a particular proposal, this is an explicit signal of the need for further consideration. The demand that a jury reach a decision, even one of marked dissensus, is another way in which it is in tension with the Habermasian formulation that relies on the possibility of revision.

The second condition (D), known as the discursive principle, contends that all who are affected by an issue must participate in the reason-giving and argumentation that precedes a decision. Such a dialogic process, the condition holds, must also rely on language that is accessible to all and not confined to experts or technocrats. Taking (D) and (U) together, Habermas presents a high standard for the legitimacy of decisions that embody the beliefs that relativism and subjectivity will not be the tragic fate of every discussion about principles and that all individuals are able to understand their interests and communicate them in a practical manner without the expectation of philosophical language.[12] (U) and (D) provide benchmarks that do not have easy correlates within the jury system: unanimity for the legitimacy of moral norms is far removed from the reality of unanimity in practical judgment and the requirement of (D), that all affected parties can participate in the discourse, also flounders given the mandate of the jury charge and the exclusion of others impacted by the crime from the process.[13] Still, it is remarkable to note that the distilled procedures for the legitimation of moral norms resemble the basic expectations for jury deliberation in ways that are unmatched by any other political or legal institution.

On the issue of consensus and legitimacy, the Supreme Court has not found the unanimity requirement to be sacrosanct, and the debate over the relative benefits and shortcomings of a unanimous decision rule over a majority one is long-standing.[14] In *Apodaca v. Oregon* the Supreme Court found that the Oregon Court of Appeals could uphold convictions by less than unanimous verdicts because unanimity is not integral to the fair and proper functioning of a trial. The Sixth Amendment guarantees the right to a speedy and fair trial with impartial jurors, but does not explicitly mention jury unanimity and this, in combination with the latitude given to the states, means that unanimity is not always the norm in the state court system (Louisiana, until recently, has been a notable outlier).[15] Further, the court found that there was no reason to believe that racial minorities would be given worse treatment in majority-rule juries than in unanimous ones. In the majority opinion, Justice White also separated the foundation of the unanimity rule from the reasonable doubt standard that crystallized after the Constitution.

Thus the requirement of unanimity is still an open question given the discretion allowed at the state level and the higher standard maintained at the federal one. The argument for unanimity hinges on the burden that it establishes, one fitting for an adversarial system of justice that takes as a hallowed value the presumed innocence of the defendant. It has also been argued that the quality of deliberation is higher when the outcome must be unanimous.[16] All participants are formally included (even if they choose to remain quiet during discussion) and the development of arguments and counterarguments is likely to be more extensive when the entire group must be convinced, not just the majority.[17] Unanimity ensures that when there is a guilty verdict all jury members are jointly responsible for such an act that authorizes the state to use force and confinement when it would otherwise be unable to do so. If a jury member is unconvinced by the evidence, then she must prevent the guilty decision from going forward, whereas in a majority-rule system, a jury member may be able to register doubt but then rationalize the outcome by claiming powerlessness to stop the guilty verdict.[18]

Habermas's argument about unanimity is not so much an additional valence to these other perspectives but a restructuring of the argument to make unanimity an essential component for legitimacy in a legal-philosophical system that is grounded in procedure and acutely aware of the systemic forces of capitalism, democratic majoritarianism, and instrumental rationality (even if he does not apply the standard to these types of institutions). The Allen Charge can be seen to compromise the ideals of the unanimity in the spirit, if not in the exact wording, of the charge. Jurors can and should be dismissed for refusal to deliberate, an act that amounts to a refusal to be part of the process of reason-giving and the adjustment of one's own ideas in light of the ideas of others. This issue is particularly salient in the case of a jury that is moving toward congealed disagreement, the kind that precipitates a discussion of the Allen Charge. If the majority is in favor of a guilty verdict and one or two jurors believe that not guilty is the appropriate verdict, they must, in the spirit of jury deliberation and Habermasian discursive principles, be willing to defend their position against arguments from the opposing side as well as to try to convince others to share their belief.[19] For those in support, the Allen Charge is an intervention specifically targeted to deter jurors from giving up on the process of deliberation.

While a refusal to deliberate or an unwillingness to consider the arguments of an opposing faction in the jury room may cause a hung jury, there may also be situations when a hung jury satisfies a preexisting belief about the fallibility of the legal process and an affirmation of the multiple valid interpretations of an event. Such is the case in the 2001 memoir of D. Graham Burnett, a historian who served as the foreman of a jury in a homicide case in New York City.[20] The case turned on the issue of self-defense; it seemed probable that the defendant killed the victim, but the circumstances surrounding the killing, including the possibility that the defendant feared he would be raped, were critical to jury deliberation. During the trial Burnett grew increasingly alienated from the prosecution's case, particularly the tone with which witnesses were questioned, as well as from the judge's manner. Yet, he did not lean toward a not guilty verdict at the beginning of the deliberation, in part because of his role as a neutral foreman and his desire to facilitate discussion, and was instead drawn to the idea of a hung jury as the outcome that would best represent his uncertainty and the inconclusive evidence. He admits that he is not entirely sure why the hung jury presented itself to him as the best option, but attributes it to an academic orientation toward evidence that sees the possibility of many narratives and the necessity of ambiguity in any interpretation. To decide on one narrative (knowing the action would precipitate sentencing or acquittal) would require from him an amount of certainty that he did not initially believe was possible based on the evidence. Nonetheless, the deliberations ended with a unanimous finding of not guilty, with leadership from Burnett. The jury provided a personalized note to the judge in addition to the decision that indicated the jurors' ambivalence toward the legal choices with which they were presented. The jury was unanimous in their decision, but less certain that the decision fit with an idealized vision of justice; their decision of not guilty did not indicate that they found the defendant entirely free from blame, just that the blame did not warrant a guilty verdict. Burnett's memoir provides an insight into yet another motivation for the hung jury, one that is consistent with the intellectual humility of academic discourse in the humanities, but one that would also be a mistake if it superseded juror responsibility to participate in deliberation about the evidence. A principled commitment to achieving a hung jury (regardless of deliberation) is just as erroneous an orientation as an excision of the option altogether.

In addition to the logic of unanimity, the condition of (D) introduces a different way of thinking about the legitimacy of consensus that can also be applied to the Allen Charge. In explaining the motivation for the Ideal Speech Situation, Habermas is animated by the possibility of creating space for political deliberation that is not primarily determined by strategic calculation. The expectation of practical discourse is in part to stave off technocratic language that acts as a veil for strategic posturing and the possibility that outcomes benefiting the few can appear to be benefiting the many. The attention to the consequences of a norm and its effect on each individual also protects against provisional acceptance of an action for future strategic play. Habermas is particularly attuned to the way in which the procedural aspects of the Ideal Speech Situation could be reduced to the bartering and domination that permeate other spheres of liberal capitalism; the demand of consensus for democratic legitimacy is a necessary antidote. The nature of jury deliberation does not encounter the long-term strategic calculations of policy debates with which Habermas is concerned, but there are incentives for jurors to act in a strategic way in order to expedite the process or increase their status in the eyes of the judge or fellow jurors. Drawing attention to the economic incentives to end deliberation with the Allen Charge gives power to the majority that is extraneous to debates about the evidence. Habermas's attention to (U) and (D) thus, through his signaling of important preconditions for discourse, suggests that the Allen Charge intercepts the trajectory of fair and impartial deliberation at a particularly vulnerable place—that of a moment where the jury may be wavering between strategic and nonstrategic deliberation. The Allen Charge introduces an element of strategic calculation into jury deliberation at a highly sensitive time when jurors are fatigued and potentially frustrated. Pressure for closure and a unanimous verdict can cause a default to the normal conditions of politics where traditional dominant groups further exert their dominance.[21] Thus, thinking with Habermas about a schematic for legitimate decision-making provides fodder for thinking about the Allen Charge as a misguided convention: one cannot justify, in the name of efficacy or closure, an intervention that threatens the standard of unanimity and the premise that all jurors have standing to participate in the process in a commensurate way. To do so would be to undermine one of the conditions that provides the greatest basis for legitimacy in the jury process.

The question of strategic discourse is not the only way discourse can be corrupted for juries; another type of distortion can emerge from restrictions on what is considered acceptable for deliberation. This is a topic where critics of Habermas, rather than Habermas himself, have made interventions that could be productively applied to the jury process. Iris Marion Young notably critiqued Habermas for his elevation of the impartial point of view over a lived, embodied, and affective one as the best perspective for reaching consensus. She sees potential in the conditions for communicative rationality but argues that Habermas's model "abstracts from the rhetorical dimensions of communication, that is, the evocative terms, metaphors, dramatic elements of the speaking, by which a speaker addresses himself or herself to this particular audience. When people converse in a concrete speaking situation, when they give and receive reasons from one another with the aim of reaching understanding, gesture, facial expression, tone of voice, as well as evocative metaphors and dramatic emphasis, are crucial aspects of their communication."[22] The openness to metaphor and contextual understanding may be more important in the cases of dramatic lifeworld differences, described below, than Habermas allows for within the context of (D) and (U).

On the Lifeworld

In addition to the centrality of (U) and (D), the Habermasian concept of the lifeworld can be persuasively enlisted for the defense of the hung jury as a legitimate and necessary outcome that deserves protection from the intervention of the Allen Charge. For Habermas, the lifeworld is the inherited world of meaning, norms, and interpretation that one gets from society and culture, and intersects with the contingencies of personality.[23] The lifeworld encompasses how one views oneself in relation to the institutions of the family, law, and the state, and it shapes intuitions about how to evaluate worth, trustworthiness, and the burden of moral action in ways that are difficult for an individual to parse. The lifeworld is one of various influences on cognitive processes and it is difficult for an individual to know just how strong its influence is. Habermas builds upon the concept of lifeworld to make two important distinctions: the first is between lifeworld and system, where the system refers to the forces of the market that impose an instrumental rationality motivated by concerns of wealth and political domination on the inherited interpretations of the lifeworld. The second distinction, of particular relevance to the deliberative process, is between the lifeworlds that participants hold and bring to the process of deliberation and the decision they are able to reach together through deliberation. He writes:

> On the one side we have the horizon of unquestioned, intersubjectively shared, nonthematized certitudes that participants in communication have

"at their backs." On the other side, participants in communication face the communicative contents constituted within a world: objects that they perceive and manipulate, norms that they observe or violate, and lived experiences to which they have privileged access and which they can express. To the extent to which participants in communication can conceive of what they reach agreement on as something in a world, something detached from the lifeworld background from which it emerged, what is explicitly known comes to be distinguished from what is implicitly certain.[24]

Thus the lifeworld is foundationally important for the process of deliberation, but successful agreement requires surrender from its deterministic aspects and the pull of tradition, culture, and the comfort of previously held coherent positions. The lifeworld for participants is what exists "at their back," yet as comprehensive as the lifeworld is, it does not prohibit communication in its fullest sense; they are able to detach the lifeworld and come to a shared understanding of the issue at hand. With this detachment comes the constructive project of explicitly creating new norms and being bound in a different way to fellow citizens. In the jury context, how jurors perceive the law and the criminal justice system, as well as their understanding of how bias and prejudice affect the law, are part of the background implied by the lifeworld. Yet, it is their belief in the integrity of the court and of the procedures in place for jury deliberation that creates the cognitive environment that enables them to decide on the facts of the case and create a shared reality distinct from the lifeworld. This is the trajectory for consensus, but *dissensus*, the less desirable outcome for both Habermas and juries, can also be seen through the lens of lifeworld. When jurors are selected, they are asked questions to determine whether they can accept the terms of the court despite the inherited forms of knowledge and assumptions that are embedded in their lifeworlds. One cannot be assumed to have abandoned previous conceptions, as the quotation above affirms, but the possibility of agreement with others within the procedural expectations of the court must be salient. In such a situation, jurors form a shared lifeworld through the immersive experience of the trial and then attempt to agree on a shared decision. They may also disagree even though they have a shared lifeworld.[25] However, given that one's lifeworld can exert a profound hold on how one understands issues such as criminality, poverty, punishment, and prejudice, it may make detachment for the sake of a shared lifeworld impossible in a given case. To put it another way, there may be cases in which differences in lifeworlds, through no fault of the court or the jurors per se, come to bear on the evidence in such a way that consensus cannot be reached.

A Conflict of Lifeworlds

It has been asserted in the secondary literature that Habermas pays in-adequate attention to theorizing the conditions when conflict cannot be transcended through consensus achieved by the procedural conditions of discourse ethics.[26] Habermas reflected on civil disobedience in the context of protests against the building of a nuclear plant and the installation of Cruise and Pershing missiles in Germany in 1981, and his position suggests parallels with the lifeworld differences I see as possible in juries.[27] Like the hung jury, civil disobedience is the last resort after all other legitimate (or in the case of juries, more highly desirable) actions have been exhausted; they can never become the default course of action if the functions of the institutions (that of the trial or the rule of law) are to be preserved. In his one speech on the topic, Habermas suggests that civil disobedience in the context of nuclear disarmament must be seen as essentially symbolic in its undermining of the legitimacy of a particular political will, and thus neither a fundamental threat to the stability provided by law nor the instantiation of a viable alternative legal order. It is interesting to note that a symbolic in-terpretation of a hung jury would be highly problematic, even for those who want to protect its legitimacy. The jury must decide on one case and one case alone. No juror should use the case at hand in order to make a larger point about the criminal justice system or about the law itself (the exception of nullification notwithstanding). A jury that is divided primarily to make a symbolic point would rankle the officers of the court and would represent just the type of mistake that proponents of the Allen Charge want to avoid.

Returning to the issue of dissensus, Habermas understood civil disobedi-ence to be the result of two different interpretations of the lifeworld. Those who opposed the creation of the nuclear plant believed that the abuse of the environment, the closed process of decision-making leading up to the policy, and the impact of the capitalist market were all systemic threats to the values of their lifeworld. Achieving a consensus with those who repre-sented this alternate set of commitments would be akin to abandoning the foundational aspects of the protesters' own lifeworld. These are the condi-tions, Habermas suggests, that call for civil disobedience and should en-gender a legitimate challenge to particular laws through direct action: "The dissensus which gains expression in this complex 'no' aims not at this or that measure or policy; it is rooted in the rejection of a life-form—namely, that life-form which has been stylized as the normal prototype—which is tailored to the needs of a capitalist modernization process, programmed for possessive individualism, for values of material security, and for the striving of competition and production, and which rests on the repression of both fear and the experience of death."[28] In such situations, saying "no" to the law and to the ideal of consensus itself emerges for Habermas as a necessary step for the further maturation of democracy and for the moral integrity of the individual who disagrees with a certain policy. A similar impasse can emerge in the jury room, where the lifeworlds of a subset of jurors converge to reject the reasoning and interpretation offered by another subset.

The conditions of universality and respect for the moral equality of each person continue to be, for Habermas, the most important checks against coercion. Stephen White and Evan Farr highlight moral equality as the linchpin that holds Habermas's theory of civil disobedience together.[29] Without the concept of moral equality, the mandate for consensus could lead the majority to insist upon compromise as evidence of good-faith deliberation. A genuine desire by the majority of jurors for the legitimacy that consensus would entail (and a belief in the reasonableness of their position) could inadvertently compromise the condition of the equality of each participant. Subsequently, the line between compromise and coercion becomes difficult to decipher. They write: "In our unorthodox account, this no-saying is not directly connected with the expectation of redemption through the achievement of rational consensus; rather, it is connected only to the expectation of some significant moral-political space being available that honors this value of the morally equal voice of each. Without this qualification, an appeal to compromises does not necessarily provide much improvement over situations of pure coercion: I agree not to shoot you, if you agree to hand over your wallet. The concept of a 'presumptively just compromise' may only be a rough standard, but it clearly disavows 'agreements' of this sort."[30] Thus the justness of an outcome, whether in compromise or dissensus, is fixed with regard to the treatment of each participant as a moral equal and one not expected to be subsumed by the desire for consensus. Were the normative weight on unanimity less, there would be greater latitude for compromises that activated strategic concerns or leveraged implicit hierarchies. Instead, to respect the morally equal voice of each, the possibility of legitimate dissensus as it emerges from irreconcilable lifeworlds must be recognized.

Lasse Thomassen further highlights that the ability to say "no" in Habermas's model is a constitutive part of understanding what it means to say "yes" in the context of consensus.[31] He extrapolates that within Habermas's discursive model, "one must interrogate the norms that constitute the 'moral-political space' of equality to find out if what appear as noise, silence, or even a 'yes' may in fact be 'no.'"[32] Similar to the point above regarding the need for heightened attention to deliberative coercion that masquerades as compromise, Thomassen suggests that there are oblique ways in which disagreement may be registered even under favorable discursive conditions. Habermas's careful elucidation of the ideal conditions for deliberation thereby provides reasons for even greater scrutiny of such phenomena and for skepticism regarding interventions such as the Allen Charge that suggest that "noise" can be ameliorated with repeated instructions. Instead, the noise and the silence to which Thomassen refers may be better understood as nascent markers of significant lifeworld differences when they appear during jury deliberation. These differences may be activated by the particularities of the case, and the same jury on a different case may not see these differences manifest, but the Habermasian insight here is the importance of deferring an interpretation until the jury itself is ready to make one. Differences in perceptions of law enforcement, the purpose of punishment, and the relationship between poverty and crime, all stemming from the lifeworlds of jurors, can be fundamental in the interpretation of evidence in a particular case, and even the best-faith attempts at deliberation cannot transcend them.[33]

The Legitimate Hung Jury

Although hung juries do not usually divide along race, it is fruitful to consider race as a factor that strongly influences one's lifeworld and could thus be significant in juries that cannot reach an agreement.[34] Judith Butler's interpretation of the Rodney King verdict provides a case study in which differences in lifeworld could have been persuasive as reasons for a hung jury. In her reflections on the case, Butler questions how a white jury could interpret the video footage of police officers beating Rodney King fifty-three times with a baton as a legitimate use of force by the officers, and she expresses her disbelief that one juror saw King as the aggressor in the situation and "in control."[35] Regarding the jury's verdict of not guilty, a decision that sparked riots in Los Angeles, Butler asserts that it is not just a matter of differences in interpretation between the jurors and others who saw the incident as embedded in racist motivations and institutional legacies. She writes:

> It is not, then, a question of negotiating between what is "seen," on the one hand, and a "reading" which is imposed upon the visual evidence, on the other. In a sense, the problem is even worse: to the extent that there is a racist organization and disposition of the visible, it will work to circumscribe what qualifies as visual evidence, such that it is in some cases impossible to establish the "truth" of racist brutality through recourse to visual evidence.

For when the visual is fully schematized by racism, the "visual evidence" to which one refers will always and only refute conditions based upon it; for it is possible within this racist episteme that no black person can seek recourse to the visible as the sure ground of evidence.[36]

In the language of the lifeworld, the differences between a lifeworld that perpetually (and perhaps unconsciously) sees the black male body as a source of threat and one that does not are not differences in interpretation of the evidence (or the part of discussion that relies on persuasion and reason-giving in a Habermasian system), but rather they emerge from the act of seeing itself. The lifeworld cannot be detached from agreement in the way Habermas suggests because it is constitutive of perception itself and consensus cannot be wrung from even the best of deliberative conditions. The Rodney King verdict shows how racial prejudices can deeply affect deliberation from the beginning and do so in ways that evade the formal protections that the jury system sets up. A hung jury in such a situation would perhaps have been a desirable outcome because it would have shown the presence of an alternative lifeworld in the jury room—one that interpreted the evidence differently and might have persuaded the other jurors or precipitated a mistrial. Even if such a juror were not able to persuade the others, the inability to reach consensus would have allowed for more time to be devoted to the case and would have perhaps involved the service of a more diverse group of jurors in another trial.

The language Butler employs when she asserts that a racist episteme can be fully determinative of how one interprets evidence is arguably the type of reasoning and strategic posturing that Habermas wants to mitigate with the right conditions for discourse. Taking the idea even further, if epistemes were all as rigid as Butler suggests, then consensus would never be possible since the entire premise of jury deliberation would be reduced to whether there is enough demographic compatibility to achieve unanimity. Hierarchies of power and audibility are real, and formal protections of unanimity and practical discourse will not be enough. It is in situations like this where the ideals Young has laid out (such as the possibilities of metaphors and embodied affect for communication) may be more effective in achieving consensus than the discursive principles Habermas suggests.[37] Consensus will not come from direct argumentation, perhaps, but from more subtle shifts in understanding others' worldviews. Habermas's understanding of the potential for agreement despite lifeworld differences is persuasive as a way to think about juries because of the jurors' commitment to the institution of the trial, the integrity of its procedures, and the gravity that comes with their ultimate decision-making authority—all of these may be synthesized into a lifeworld and decision-making process that resonate with all. Yet, Butler's sharp assessment of the proceedings of the Rodney King trial draws much-needed attention to the potential legitimacy of disagreement in the jury box and the ways formal protections of the deliberative process can be impotent in the face of injustice, bias, and coercion.

The language of *belief* in the Allen Charge, as well as the suggestion that holdout jurors are not cooperating in the deliberative process, suggests that it is a matter of conscience that is preventing a juror from being convinced, and this is not always accurate or desirable. Drawing upon Habermas's understanding of the lifeworld and Butler's language of the racist episteme points to something more systematic than a discrete belief in the mind of a holdout radically enfranchised juror. The inability to achieve consensus with other jurors may not be because an individual cannot shake a doubt that exceeds what is reasonable; it may be the result of a more comprehensive difference in how she views and interprets evidence and the pressures that motivate citizens and law enforcement.[38] Still, the radically enfranchised juror will not foreclose the possibilities for consensus at the gate; she will proceed through deliberations with attention to the rights of the defendant and the conventions of the trial, as well as with an attitude of generosity toward her fellow jurors. If comprehensive worldview differences emerge, including in the basic assumptions about visibility, the radically enfranchised juror is still tasked with making the best case for what justice would entail but is concurrently aware of the epistemological value of the hung jury.

The fact that Habermas has been accused of not giving adequate attention to legitimate conflict is related to the additional critique that he fails to consider specific issues that arise in the formation of the lifeworld for marginal members of the citizenry, those who do not fit into dominant conceptions of gender or race, for example. Nancy Fraser's critique of Habermas for his lack of attention to the ways in which women's consent during deliberation is misunderstood and misconstrued in both the public and private spheres is meant to point to the fragility of the deliberative space from the perspective of women, despite the fact that they are necessary for the "universalization" Habermas desires.[39] Fraser writes that the consent women give, in sexual situations and others, can be willfully and violently misread, such that an agentic act becomes a passive one (e.g., when "no" is interpreted to mean "yes"), and her critique can be broadened to include the dangers of formal proceduralism obscuring the dynamics of power within jury deliberation. Fraser's critique suggests that racial minority jurors who also make up the minority on the jury decision are even more vulnerable to having their perspectives obscured in light of the desire for consensus. The very fact that each juror must register an opinion, not just give tacit consent or remain neutral, is a worthy protection against the problems of traditionally marginalized voices within Habermas's model.

Furthermore, Fraser's concern about the incorporation of the perspective of women within the Ideal Speech Situation also centers on the distinction Habermas draws between the system and lifeworld (with concerns of the material world and the labor of the household falling under the rubric of system). Fraser suggests that for traditionally marginalized groups, such a distinction is incongruous and their relationship to labor is the basis for lifeworld, not an oppositional force within it. Following from this, we can surmise that the way the lifeworld influences decisions in the context of a jury may not always follow the stark demarcation that Habermas would like. The interlocking concerns of system and lifeworld, especially in the case of certain groups, can become salient in jury deliberation and be a factor in divergent lifeworlds. Recognition of the validity of such an impasse is also a constructive response to the reality that power relations in society can be replicated within the jury room and require a heightened degree of protection to maintain the conditions of deliberation.

One might counter that the Allen Charge is merely restating expectations that were given in the original jury charge. If the language of the charge suggests the need for consideration of the strategic values of expediency and the expectation that the jury follow certain procedures for deliberation, and these guidelines are coercive, this is a problem with the original charge itself and broader reforms should be made to the jury system. The Allen Charge, the argument might go, is only a reminder at a critical time of the accepted responsibilities of the jury. If it encourages further debate toward the end of consensus, this is a net gain. If not, the jury is not worse off than when they approached the judge or were otherwise perceived to be on the cusp of deadlock. Yet, what Habermas's theory reveals is the need to protect the conditions of deliberation at each stage, particularly against the corruption of the goals of the process and in the service of the equal respect that is granted to each participant. The fact that there are obstacles toward achieving the Habermasian ideals of unanimity and equal participation does not mean they are irrelevant or in need of replacement. Rather, his philosophical defense of discourse ethics alongside his understanding of the reality of lifeworld differences provides a way to understand the significance of the hung jury (and the error of the Allen Charge). It is interesting to note that in simulated jury studies, majority jurors were more likely to exercise influence in the jury room after an Allen Charge and were emboldened to assert the veracity of their position. Even though all jurors were equally advised to reconsider their positions, the intervention of the judge through the Allen Charge fortified the majority position and gave the majority the impression that they had the support of the judge in moving to consensus.[40] This was especially true when the case hinged on issues of values and judgments, rather than technical concerns. Specifically, Martin Kaplan and Charles Miller found that normative pressures from the majority predominated in juries that were discussing questions of values and personal standards, whereas information influence was more important in juries that decided on issues of facts.[41] Their research found that juries "in cases that involve community and moral standards (e.g. those that involve obscenity, abortion, police brutality, euthanasia or political dissent)" may be more susceptible to the influence of the Allen Charge.[42] While Habermas would be hopeful that consensus could be achieved even in these types of cases through fair and impartial deliberation (and in even broader situations of norm legitimation than is generally sought through jury decisions), I have argued that cases that fail to reach consensus may sometimes be grounded in these types of lifeworld differences, not on a willful failure to deliberate or an incompetence regarding the evidence (though the confidentiality of jury deliberation makes it hard to know), and it is beneficial for the radically enfranchised juror to be aware of this possibility. Thus, the Allen Charge empowers majority jurors to exert further normative influence in precisely the types of cases that are likely to activate different understandings of the lifeworld. The Rodney King case did not turn on the issue of an Allen Charge, but I invoke it to show how fragile lifeworld positions in the jury might be when there is an overwhelming alternative (especially a prejudiced one). Juries that have reached an impasse may not be the cases that should have their deliberation hastened for the sake of efficiency; these are the cases likely to be manifestations of a legitimate hung jury and not the mistake.

Understanding the Allen Charge as a mistaken attempt to achieve the ideal of unanimity is consistent with the change in judge-jury relations suggested in the discussion of Tocqueville and Lieber that will be described in chapter 4. An orientation of radical enfranchisement does not follow the unidirectional model of the omniscient judge and jurors perpetually in need of education. Especially at the end of the deliberation period, jurors should understand themselves as having the responsibilities and powers of radical enfranchisement, including a degree of autonomy from the interests of the judge and the officers of the court in relation to the verdict. Radical enfranchisement is, in part, a recognition of the divergence in perceptions of justice between jurors and the repeat players of the criminal justice process. Jurors are the ones who have not seen it all before, and, to this end, are better able to be attentive to the particularity of this defendant, these facts, and the value of punishment in these circumstances. The Allen Charge obscures this function of the jury.

A Mistake or a Brake?

The controversies over the Allen Charge can be seen as the dueling dangers of two types of mistakes. The first is the mistake of a coercive action by the court that upsets the delicate balance of the jury deliberation process for the sake of a unanimous verdict. The second mistake in question is that of the hung jury. The hung jury results in a mistrial and prolongs the criminal justice process such that it may extend to another trial or plea-bargaining. From the perspective of efficiency, a hung jury is suboptimal and arguably a "mistake" precipitated by the actions of the judge or attorneys. A hung jury can also be seen as a mistake if jurors refuse to partake in the work of argument, interpretation, and persuasion on the questions of evidence and the burden of proof. This is not the case in juries that are divided because of substantial lifeworld differences that make shared interpretation of the evidence impossible. Jurors in cases like these cannot step away from their lifeworld interpretation in order to achieve consensus. To be true to their understanding of the case and their responsibilities as jurors, they must risk being seen by others as the holdouts who contribute to a mistrial. In addition, from the perspective of justice writ large, the hung jury should also be seen as a hand brake on the punishment component of the criminal justice system, a component widely documented to be vexed by racial and socio-economic inequality. When a system is as flawed as the US criminal justice system, an outcome that may at first seem like a mistake of inefficiency (and worthy of an explicit remedy such as the Allen Charge) might better be thought of as a type of immanent resistance delivered at precisely the moment the state has the greatest leverage over the defendant—the moment of the guilty verdict.

THREE

No One but You:
Jurors and the Internal Standard
of Reasonable Doubt

"Nice bunch of guys, eh?"

"They're about the same as everyone else."

—*12 Angry Men* (1957)

In Franz Kafka's parable *Before the Law* a man approaches the gates of the Law and tries to seek entrance from the gatekeeper.[1] He is denied and does not know why. For years he tries to cajole and bribe the gatekeeper in order to have access to one of the highest sources of authority he knows. The gatekeeper accepts the gifts because he knows how important it is for the man to believe that he is doing everything possible to achieve entrance even though his attempts are misguided. When the man is on his deathbed, he asks the gatekeeper why no one else has entered the gate in all these years. The gatekeeper, frustrated at his appetite and his ineptitude, shouts at him, "Here no one else can gain entry, since this entrance was assigned only to you. I'm going now to close it." The parable appears in *The Trial* and seems to confirm that the nightmare of false accusations, bureaucracy, and faceless authority will ultimately overwhelm each person in their own unique way. It is also about how the law will perpetually thwart the aspirations of the unsophisticated man who misses the expectation of self-transformation and fails to realize that the power of the law comes from seeing oneself as its author. Without adequately preparing oneself to judge, including taking account of one's own shortcomings, one will never be able to exercise authority justly. This is particularly true for the juror tasked with becoming the final arbiter in a court of law. While this responsibility appears to require only adherence to rules and external standards, it also requires an internal transformation in the process of judgment for each juror—*This entrance was assigned only to you*. Accepting this responsibility for a transformation of judgment and the way it is connected to the biases, prejudices, and vulnerabilities each juror brings to a trial should be seen as a secondary valence of the standard of reasonable doubt. As the standard for the extremely high burden of proof on the state necessary for a guilty verdict, the phrase "beyond a reasonable doubt" is the quintessential legal convention that jurors may have heard about before entering the courtroom and are mandated to reckon with during deliberation. What is less familiar is a connection that could be made between the juror's role in interpreting the standard and the tools that the process gives them for an assessment of their *own* decision making. Kafka's parable captures how failing to internalize certain aspects of the law prevents a juror from entering the gate at all.

On Implicit Bias

"He refused to testify so he must be guilty."
"People like her lie on the witness stand."
"If he didn't do it, why is he on trial?"

Each of these statements represents a plausible snap judgment of a juror who may be aspiring to impartiality, as her role requires, but who cannot help but make prejudicial assessments of the defendants and witnesses in the courtroom. Mere admonishment to be fair will likely not change a juror's mind about these assumptions, but perhaps the internalization of reasonable doubt will usher in an approach to a juror's *own* judgment that can be used to counter bias in its many forms. There is perhaps no more potent critique of the jury system at the present moment than its complicity in a racist institution, one in which the inferior, often violent, treatment given to African-Americans and others is systemic and present in each stage of the criminal justice system.[2] The jury process may be seen as a particularly vile node within this system because of the way it uses laypeople to legitimize decisions about punishment that are consistent with discriminatory practices. Increasing evidence about the reality of implicit bias, hidden biases that do not invalidate jury service, in contrast to the outcome of openly racist responses during voir dire, has only complicated perceptions of the integrity of jury decisions. Applying the ideals of reasonable doubt to the perceptions of jurors themselves in relation to both the factual and moral questions embedded in the charge is one way to highlight how critical the task of self-assessment is, equal to external engagement with the evidence.

Using the term "doubt" rather than "critical thinking" better evokes the destabilization that accompanies the process for jurors. The cognitive uncertainty that comes with doubting the shortcuts to which one has grown accustomed should cause even those who think of themselves as critical thinkers to pause. Doubt is the action that disrupts *doxa*, the unexamined norms circulating within a community, and they include norms about criminality, the police, and stereotypical characteristics of defendants. While we are all shaped by doxa, one might argue that it is those jurors who are most certain of their capacity to render judgment in an impartial way that have the most to gain from turning the standard inward. They may be overly confident that they can navigate the standards of the law and the judge's expectations, but they have perhaps not thought about how the standard narratives that give coherence to their understandings of justice, doxa that they have integrated into their own perspective, might be misleading for the case at hand.

This chapter will examine the history of the jury and the way jurors have been both celebrated for their "insider knowledge" of the case and then later disqualified when they have any awareness of the crime. Turning doubt inward is one way to clarify how jurors can best use the intuitions, life experiences, and community knowledge that they bring to the courtroom. To that end, I will look at what the concept of doubt can bring to the practice of being a juror and the way that it acts as a bridge between intuition and practical wisdom for jurors. Lastly, I will attend to how foregrounding doubt as an attitude for the individual can have consequences for the deliberations of the jury as a whole.

On the Evolution of Reasonable Doubt

The United States has an adversarial system of criminal justice in which the presumption of innocence means that the burden of proof to show guilt is entirely on the state. The defendant does not have to prove that she is innocent; anything less than the strongest of cases presented by the state should lead to a finding of not guilty, a standard evoked because of the gravity of the consequences for individual liberty if the defendant is convicted.[3] The 1987 pattern jury charge enunciated by the Federal Judicial Center is one explanation of the threshold of certainty implied by the reasonable doubt standard:

> Proof beyond a reasonable doubt is proof that leaves you firmly convinced of the defendant's guilt. There are very few things in this world that we know with absolute certainty, and in criminal cases the law does not require proof

that overcomes every possible doubt. If, based on your consideration of the evidence, you are firmly convinced that the defendant is guilty of the crime charged, you must find him guilty. If on the other hand, you think there is a real possibility that he is not guilty, you must give him the benefit of the doubt and find him not guilty.[4]

For many who have not served as jurors or trained in the law, this is a remarkably vague set of instructions. It gives no examples or tests, nor does it seem to warn jurors against the prejudices that they harbor, but the standard does in fact provide a way to think about them. Allowing for the power of self-authorship by the jurors themselves, it leaves the exact meaning of "reasonable doubt" open for contestation in the jury room with the hope that such debate will be beneficial to the deliberation on the verdict itself.[5]

In common usage, doubt is often described as uneasiness, or a sense that something is not right on a "gut level," and the speaker cannot say exactly what factors (and there are usually many) are contributing to it. The advice to "sleep on" a difficult decision and see how one feels when one wakes up is also meant to get at the combination of affective and pragmatic concerns that accompany complex decisions with uncertain outcomes. The same admixture of assessments and affects is relevant to a juror or a jury as a whole as they put together questions about the credibility of the witnesses and the evidence presented. No one aspect of a testimony may seem patently false, but together there may be a pattern of distortion or dissemblance that is strong enough to constitute severe weakness in the prosecution's case. Turning the reasonable doubt standard inward asks jurors to apply a similar type of scrutiny to all the decisions they make prior to the verdict. Just as the reasonable doubt standard is meant to make explicit to jurors that a mere "hunch" that someone is guilty is not enough to convict, turning the standard inward provides an additional mechanism to interrogate the influences that may be wrongly shaping the juror's opinion in the steps leading up to the ultimate question.

In the inquisitorial process of the Roman trial, the early precursor to the jury system as we know it, the court used a formula: two reliable witnesses or a confession by the defendant would result in the finding of guilt. While such a parsimonious calculation may now seem ripe for abuse and falsification by the state, it attempted to take the subjectivity of court officers out of the process in its own way, just as contemporary procedures try to do. Later, in the medieval period when the jury emerged as a fixture of the trial, its legal value was located in the jurors' particular knowledge of the people and facts relevant to the case. They were, in a manner of speaking, experts in the society in which the crime had taken place. It was precisely their partiality and knowledge of the reputations of their neighbors that was valuable, not their ability to separate themselves from these instincts. Marianne Constable has shown that such expertise in jurors was so esteemed in the English courts of the Middle Ages that when the defendant was a foreigner or from a particular guild, such as that of the merchants, it was necessary to find jurors with similar backgrounds.[6] The "mixed jury," as she has described it, is a testament to how the integrity of the trial depended on whether or not a defendant was judged by a true jury of peers who had firsthand knowledge of the social context and the customary laws that governed action. The assumption that foreigners were desirable for these trials evinces an awareness by officers of the court that local jurors might not only lack this specific knowledge (doxa) but might also be unduly prejudiced against the defendant. Constable highlights the ways in which the mixed jury was a recognition that justice required more than an adherence to a positivist conception of the law, social norms, and local knowledge; sympathy for the defendant should also be considered. On the evolution of the jury trial since that time, she writes,

> A strange inversion has occurred: where once all were insiders of communities who knew their own law, all are now observers of a world that posits truth of fact. In place of the community's knowledge of what to do appear sciences of society and government, whose truths inform the judgments of state officials. The community has been turned inside out under a gaze that makes aliens of us all.[7]

One of the reasons why "the community has been turned inside out" is the fear of the ways community knowledge can become a cover for prejudicial opinions and parochial understandings of who and what represent the community. In the twentieth century, the convergence of a belief in the technorationalist power of the state (through forensic technology) with the discrediting of jurors, particularly during the Jim Crow and civil rights eras, has left the jury in a debilitated position. Yet Constable's formulation helps to show the stakes when we completely give up on the jury as entrusted with navigating changing norms from the inside. For a defendant to lose the opportunity to be judged by her peers because we do not know either who should be considered peers or none are able to fairly judge is an impossible price to pay. Instead, the integrity of the jury trial depends on cultivating practical wisdom about punishment while being realistic about the impediments to juror fairness and impartiality.

The increasing social and legal complexity of trials during the seventeenth and eighteenth centuries prompted witnesses to become more integral to the workings of the trial, and jurors were now called to evaluate the testimony of witnesses who brought specialized knowledge to the case. Yet assessing the credibility of witnesses, then as now, is still a determination that cannot be reduced to a formulaic calculation. It requires jurors to navigate between judgment based on prejudice and considered reflection. It demands valuations from jurors based on character details, demographic information, and their own anecdotal experiences—a process that is much better pursued by a group of laypeople than a singular entity because of the need to consider a high number of relevant factors.[8] Whether or not one trusts a witness is likely to depend not only on errors of fact or outright deception but on other verbal and nonverbal cues as well as the affective response a juror has to a witness. The historical trajectory of the jury has thus created a conundrum for jurors today: they are neither confident in their status as peers of the defendant and what that implies for judgment nor, because of what we know about implicit bias, are they able to be unbiased outsiders who have the skills or training to counter erroneous assumptions. A turning inward of the standard of reasonable doubt is one way to try to remedy the problem and enhance the community judgment function that is so crucial to the legitimacy of punishment.

The reasonable doubt standard emerged in the history of political thought alongside an Enlightenment investigation into what the increasing rationality of the scientific method meant for knowledge about social and political systems. Within the criminal trial, the transformation from jurors' firsthand knowledge of evidence to their assessments of witness credibility paralleled the split between empirical or mathematical knowledge that could be proven with absolute certainty or verified by the senses, and the type of learning (by observation and probability) about people and events that was preoccupying the great thinkers of the time. Francis Bacon and John Locke, both concerned about the implications of advances in scientific rationalism for other types of knowledge, were interested in the possibility of differentiating between degrees of certainty and the ability of language to capture these differences in a meaningful way. Bacon celebrated the jury as one of the jewels in the crown of the English legal system and compared the task of juries to that of the most discerning kings.[9] The air of responsibility held by jurors and the institution itself ennobled the role of laypeople. For Bacon, no part of the jury's task could be performed mechanically, and it was the act of deciding under difficult and even contradictory conditions that made the task so important for the legal process. It was up to the consciences and "private knowledge" of juries to decide on "both the supply of testimony and the discerning and credit" of it.[10]

John Locke's "An Essay Concerning Human Understanding" (1689) develops a bimodal theory of knowledge based either in (1) sensory information or (2) cognitive reflection, with the latter necessary for distinguishing between opinion and knowledge in the realm of human affairs. Locke delineates the different levels of confidence: from doubt to probability to certainty, and then, finally, to knowledge, which can only be achieved with one's senses.[11] Doubt is therefore not an all-encompassing term for every orientation that falls short of knowledge, but is rather a strategic way to asymptotically propel one's opinion toward knowledge. An educated man should achieve competence, and even a degree of precision, in accurately assessing what level of uncertainty he holds and what might be required to get to a higher level without the benefit of sensory confirmation. In the contemporary context, he must also be aware of the ways that confidence in one's powers of observation and deduction by probability can be skewed to the point of inaccuracy. By moving up the steps of intuition, hesitation, doubt, and knowledge, one could get closer to certainty while still acknowledging personal fallibility and the unknowability of the event itself. While the exact margins of certainty were debatable, Locke's argument placed tremendous faith in the accuracy of terminology to serve as the basis upon which individual assessments could converge regarding certainty in nonempirical matters. His schematic shows an attempt to erect a breakwall of definitions against the tides of subjectivity, and the turning inward of the standard of reasonable doubt can be seen in a similar manner.

By the seventeenth century, the determination of certainty in reference to testimony and the quality of evidence takes on an affective or motivational component, apparent in the particular phrases—"If you believe," "If you are satisfied with the evidence," and the presence of "a satisfied conscience"— that appear repeatedly in legal codes as guidelines for convictions by a jury.[12] The phrases do not reference an external standard of assessment, nor do they talk about the aggregate opinions of the group, but refer to the disposition of the juror as the standard for assessing guilt. For the contemporary juror it is this affective component of the resolution of doubt that may be hastening the internal scrutiny jurors should undertake; they feel satisfied with their judgment even though they have not gone through the destabilizing process of doubt. Jurors may be skipping the dialectical process that proceeds from intuition to doubt to enhanced judgment and reaching the point of satisfaction too quickly. To be "satisfied" with one's decision is to achieve a stasis regarding the internal conflict of constantly wanting more information or more effective persuasion in order to make a decision. Before the point of satisfaction, the juror should have asked many questions about the evidence and the credibility of the witnesses as well as an equal number about her own judgments. The adversarial exchange between the prosecution and the defense in the courtroom may be replicated internally within each juror as she considers the evidence and competing narratives, but the juror must eventually be able to determine for herself, and with the group, whether or not the state has met its extraordinarily high burden of proof. Turning the reasonable doubt standard inward also means meeting the other high standard that one has, to the best of her ability, tried to correct the judgments that emerged from biases or shortcuts in thinking.

What is gained through the language of doubt when we talk about turning it inward? The experience of doubt as part of the process of thinking was once described by John Dewey as a "shock of coolness" that generates "confusion and suspended belief," and his description captures that doubt is an uneasy physical state, where we are discomfited by our thoughts and the conventional ways we resolve inconsistencies in judgments.[13] We will be tempted to quickly recalibrate the situation to our liking by reverting to a previous assumption and taking comfort in a worldview we know others like us will understand. Practicing doubt in regard to our internal judgments is fundamentally destabilizing, and while jurors may be accustomed to such an orientation in relation to the facts of the case, they may not realize that it should also happen in relation to instinctual judgments. The destabilization that comes with turning doubt inward is not the result of conflictual fact patterns but of the awareness that the shortcuts in thinking that structure much of everyday life cannot hold when jurors are asked to render judgment on the actions of particular defendant.

Turning the reasonable doubt standard inward can be understood as analogous to the shift between the System 1 and System 2 modes of thought that psychologist Daniel Kahneman has described.[14] In his heuristic, System 1 thoughts are the fast, intuitive judgments that make up much of daily life and are shortcuts to thinking, especially when we are afraid or anxious. Stereotypes are the most complex form of System 1 thought because they require the synthesis of different observations in one instantaneous judgment about a complex issue (a person's character, for example). System 2 thought requires more effort, higher level reasoning, and self-reflection. Through extra labor, System 2 thought may allow us to counter some of the biases that creep in when the snap decisions of System 1 thought are made. For jurors, it would seem that the demands of service would necessarily require System 2 modes of thought: there is too much information to be processed to do it quickly, and the law is exacting. Yet, perhaps the very conditions of the trial and the type of focused thinking that jurors are asked to do, day after day, lead to shortcuts in evaluation. Turning reasonable doubt inward is a way to think about how System 2 thinking must be brought to bear during come critical moments in the determination of the verdict despite the pressures to make decisions efficiently. Kahneman is a realist about human nature and knows that nudges can only go so far in changing human behavior, but his framework suggests that a juror's desire to make more informed decisions can be harnessed at different points in the trial. Namely, turning reasonable doubt inward could serve as a means of scrutiny for the ways jurors maintain an active presumption of innocence, evaluate the testimony of witnesses, and resist the seductions of narrative closure. Each of these areas is ripe for incomplete intuitive assessments, but the act of doubting, with its affective and cognitive dimensions, can lead to better acts of judgment.

Turning doubt inward and then using the experience of examining one's instincts and previously held assumptions as the basis for interacting with fellow jurors is a critical step in moving from initial reactions to doubt to a type of practical wisdom. Turning doubt inward requires that one take the framework of the court seriously as an incubator for applied thought. Within the structure of the trial, the adversarial process requires independent thought to determine the verdict, the unanimity requirement ensures that each juror's opinion is included, and the privacy of jury deliberations reflects the utmost trust in the ability of citizens, selected by lot, to determine whether punishment is warranted. The strangeness of the surroundings and the invocation of rules contributes to a juror feeling like she is out of sync with the rest of her life, a desirable state given the importance of self-scrutiny. The orientation expected from jurors is not that they set aside common sense or the benefits of life experience for making judgments about character, motivation, and guilt, but that they are willing to concede that additional scrutiny is necessary and that the trial provides concrete opportunities to do so. It is also a change in self-conception from certainty in one's initial assessments to a stance of humility about what one needs to learn about the particularities of the case and, ultimately, a regained confidence in the ability to make the right decision about the verdict.

Dewey gives us a language for considering what practical wisdom after doubt might look like when he writes, "No hard and fast rules for this operation of selecting and rejecting, or fixing upon the facts, can be given. It all comes back, as we say, to the good judgment, the good sense, of the one judging. To be a good judge is to have a sense of the relative indicative or signifying values of the various features of the perplexing situation; to know what to let go as of no account; what to eliminate as irrelevant; what to retain as conducive to outcome; what to emphasize as a clue to the difficulty."[15] Even after a juror has accounted for difficulties maintaining the presumption of innocence, better crediting witnesses, and openness to alternative narratives, there will still be conflicting evidence and the challenge of knowing, as Dewey writes, what to retain as conducive to the outcome given the gravity of the decision. Turning doubt inward does not imply that jurors forever question their ability to offer a verdict because of a lack of confidence. Rather the process narrows the chasm of bias in a way that helps turn attention to relevant aspects of the case including the factual and moral.

Turning doubt inward is a necessary step in the engagement with epistemic peers during jury deliberation. Preparing for the likelihood that one is mistaken, an assumption one makes in a disagreement with someone who is considered an epistemic peer, is a critical step in believing that others are necessary to reach the best verdict. While deliberations are not monitored and not expected to be "run" in any formal way by the foreperson or anyone else, radically enfranchised jurors expect that there will be ample opportunity for all jurors to speak, even if this means having more formal systems in place (such as a list of speakers). More importantly though, the radically enfranchised juror realizes that turning doubt inward goes hand in hand with attention to the opinions of other jurors.

Turning reasonable doubt inward may also bolster the types of effects scholars have claimed from racially diverse juries.[16] An orientation of doubt toward the assumptions one brings into the courtroom and a sense that assessments of character and credibility are especially prone to bias is a necessary step in avoiding a replication of status hierarchies within the jury room and a verdict tainted by prejudice. Studies have shown the jurors in racially mixed juries display greater anxiety and self-monitoring, but also greater time spent on deliberation.[17] This combination of anxiety and self-monitoring is similar to what may happen with the turning inward of doubt. Conducting an experiment with white mock jurors who deliberated online (in either all white or racially mixed juries) and then subjecting their discussion to a linguistic analysis, Margaret Stevenson et al. find, "Mock jurors engaged in greater information-search efforts (used more question marks, more third-person pronouns, and more inclusion words) when the holdout juror was Black than when he was White."[18] While the racial makeup is offered as the cause for better techniques of discussion, an orientation of radical enfranchisement puts the responsibility on individual jurors to act in this way aside from the characteristics of the group. The scrutiny required of a radically enfranchised juror depends more on (1) a realization of the potential for bias in so many judgments made during a trial and (2) the gravity of the verdict, not primarily on fear of appearing to be racist in a racially mixed jury.

An Active Presumption

While the adversarial system is based on a presumption of innocence in order to keep the focus on the burden of the state to make its case of guilt, jurors are often much more familiar and comfortable with a presumption of guilt. As Ralph Grunewald writes, "In narratological terms, within the (ideal typical) crime control framework, the story of a guilty suspect is archetypical. Once the presumption of guilt is established (early in the process), the innocence story becomes an atypical and unlikely story. Because of the operational confidence in the screening process that is conducted by the police, it is assumed that a defendant is typically guilty."[19] The archetypal story of guilt is further strengthened by the fact that this particular person was considered worthy of standing trial by a grand jury or judicial action. Because of the evidence collected the defendant is, in an important way, in a much more vulnerable situation than the juror, a difference that may make it difficult for a juror to maintain the presumption of innocence. Turning reasonable doubt inward suggests that the presumption of innocence is something that jurors can learn to do, rather than something that they are merely expected to keep in mind.[20] Maintaining the presumption of innocence requires jurors to bring a level of scrutiny to the judgments they make throughout the trial that may be reliant on assumptions of guilt. To help with this task I follow Richard Lippke, R. A. Duff, and others in advocating for informing the jury of what a presumption of innocence means at the beginning of the trial, a reminder that will be more effective if it echoes what potential jurors learn through civic education.[21] Jurors should be told that the defendant should be viewed as a law-abiding individual and all claims should be evaluated in that light.[22] Such a statement conveys an explicit framing of a juror's orientation toward the defendant in contradistinction to the observations a juror may have made based on pretrial conditions of detention, publicity, stereotypes, or any other factor. While clarifying the meaning of the presumption to a jury can be beneficial, whether it will actually take hold in a juror's judgment requires an internalization of doubt. Jurors should also interrogate their assumptions in the situation where the defendant invokes her Fifth Amendment privilege not to self-incriminate.[23] To many jurors this is not an intuitive right; in 1968 Judge Henry Friendly famously challenged the justification for protections against self-incrimination when he wrote, "Every hour of the day people are being asked to explain their conduct to parents, employers and teachers. Those who are questioned consider themselves to be morally bound to respond."[24] Yet, the context of a criminal trial is different from everyday life, and the privilege is consistent with the acknowledged reality of the power that a state may bring to bear (through the police and the courts) on a citizen when attempting to convict.[25] While the presumption of innocence may be diminished as a juror is persuaded by evidence and testimony, it must be made salient by jurors in the deliberation room with jurors asking themselves if their interpretation of evidence would change if they treated the defendant as an innocent person.

For example, the presumption of innocence may be distorted by misunderstandings by the jury about what the presence of remorse indicates. When defendants take the stand, they open themselves up to cross-examination as well as information about past criminal history, but each has the rare opportunity to become a more fully realized person in the eyes of the jury. Anecdotes of jurors being moved to compassion for the defendant often turn on such events, which include the opportunity for the defendant to express remorse. The question of remorse is complicated, however, by the fact that remorse often does not sound like what jurors' expect to hear and can be interpreted as insufficient, manipulative, or insincere. While children are not usually tried before juries, an investigation into how remorse is perceived when children are accused of a crime is instructive. Martha Grace Duncan's examination of cases with child defendants suggests that laypeople often do not have the psychological tools for understanding the complex reasons why a child may not show remorse, including a failure to see the permanence of their actions. What children say does not necessarily lead others to more accurate decisions about their culpability or capacity for rehabilitation.[26]

Turning reasonable doubt inward is similar to what Sherman Clark called the "moral discomfort" device of the presumption of innocence.[27] It is not enough to focus on the interpretation of evidence when applying the standard of the presumption of innocence; a juror should also attribute the characteristics that they associate with an "innocent" person to the defendant, a difficult task in light of the fact that there is only one person on trial before them. Clark emphasizes the weight of responsibility of judgment, a task meant to cause a type of internal reckoning and, in his eyes, a healthy sense that one is not worthy to judge because of how much the defendant shares with all the others that society deems innocent. It is plausible that a juror may, if taking fully into account the presumption of innocence, want to avoid the task of judgment, but Clark characterizes the potential for growth and courage that comes along with it. It is precisely because judgment is difficult and requires that jurors "feel and carry" the burden that it becomes a counterweight to the types of judgment that may initially be marked by bias and therefore a necessary step to the self-authorship of the law that jury service enables.[28]

Narrative and the Jury

It is a cliché of legal pedagogy that cases are won and lost through storytelling. The brilliant orator in the courtroom could be the prosecuting attorney who can weave the facts of the case, the law, and the moral gravity of the crime into a mandate to the jury to convict, or the defense attorney whose narrative of misplaced blame or unconscionable duress elicits outrage or mercy. In an influential article describing how jurors use narratives to reach a decision, Nancy Pennington and Reid Hastie write, "the Story Model includes the following three components: (a) evidence evaluation through story construction, (b) representation of the decision alternatives by learning verdict category attributes, and (c) reaching a decision through the classification of the story into the best-fitting verdict category," where jurors take into account the "coverage, coherence, uniqueness, and goodness-of-fit" allowed by the narrative.[29] The ability to persuade a jury that one's story is the most compelling interpretation of the event requires that an attorney organize the vast swath of evidence and interpretation into a favorable cognitive frame or "schema," using all rhetorical skills at her disposal.[30] While the story model is persuasive, it also points to its own limitations as part of what Roland Barthes described as the potentially unseemly exchange between justice and literature.

In 1952, Dominici, an eighty-year-old farmer in Provence, France, was sentenced to death for killing Sir Jack Drummond and his family, a conviction Roland Barthes argues was only made possible by writerly conventions, including "antithesis, metaphors, flights of oratory," which the judge and the prosecutors convincingly deployed to malign the defendant.[31] The language used to try Dominici activated accrued tropes and prejudices such that form and content merged to convey a familiar narrative of a guilty man. Barthes writes, "Justice and literature have made an alliance, they have exchanged their old techniques, thus revealing their basic identity, and compromising each other barefacedly." It is an awareness of this exchange that I see as part of the radical enfranchisement of jurors, a reorientation of juror power to scrutinize not just the evidence but the inherited frameworks that shape a juror's understandings of how to interpret it.[32] Even in the absence of extreme behavior, turning reasonable doubt inward demands the sensitivity of jurors to the dangers of accepting the story model. For jurors to consider the possibility of innocence, they must avoid turning to doxa and filling in gaps in the story with established scripts of prejudices.[33] Thus, turning reasonable doubt inward means that a juror should forgo implicitly adding the information that would make a narrative of guilt cohere, especially those details that would aide in the juror's moral comfort. This is a task demanding of practical wisdom and one that would benefit from multiple exposures to its challenges. Jurors must investigate whether the stories that are scaffolding their thinking about the case may be concealing various types of biases, including the bias that a not guilty verdict suggests that they are not taking seriously the fact that a violation occurred and requires that the offender be punished.

The narratives presented to the jury can be understood as a type of ur-narrative, related to the primary historical function of narrative itself and satisfying a need for legal and moral order in light of a disruptive event.[34] Yet, the challenge arises when there is a disjuncture between a jury's desire to account for the historical event, the crime, and two flawed narratives.[35] The demand of a jury to measure the prosecutorial narrative against the standard of showing guilt beyond a reasonable doubt, an abstract task, may be interrupted by a desire to account for the crime in a plausible way. The defense narrative may be partially effective in sowing the seeds of doubt, but it cannot offer what the jury may ultimately want: a narrative of another defendant. This *third narrative*, the shadow story, could be the one that provides the meaning and coherence which makes the sequence of events leading to the crime and its aftermath legible, but it is never part of the trial.[36] The most dangerous implication of the lack of a third narrative is the way it can muddle assessments of reasonable doubt; the doubt surrounding guilt that a jury sees in the narrative laid forth by the state becomes distorted because of the jury's desire to conclude the case in a morally satisfying way. One of the skills of doubting when it comes to the jurors themselves is openness to imagining the third narrative of a crime. Hayden White argues that the open-ended history of annals, rather than the closure-seeking one of narratives, often elicits the same sort of frustrations that I see in the jury without access to a third narrative. Chronicles as a genre provide a satisfying moralistic ending, but White shows how much of the hope for narrative is perhaps wrongly tethered to a "desire to have real events display the coherence, integrity, fullness, and closure of an image of life that is and can only be imaginary."[37] As Pennington and Hastie show in their experimental work, juries too must grapple with this desire for a narrative of coherence and integrity and should sometimes resist the pull of the fragmented narrative as the best option, but not so much so that only DNA evidence is considered persuasive enough for a guilty verdict (as happens with the "CSI effect").[38] An orientation of turning doubt inward would be one that acknowledges, but ultimately resists, the allure of closure that a prosecutorial narrative provides, especially given the challenges for jurors of assessing guilt in light of the vagueness and flexibility present in the reasonable doubt standard.[39]

There are, of course, people who are very invested in manipulating a jury's understanding of a narrative—these are the attorneys and the trial consultants they hire who often employ an arsenal of sophisticated psychological and rhetorical tools to get the verdict they want.[40] For example, practicing attorney Bruce B. Whitman has written a book for plaintiffs in civil suits teaching them how to persuade juries to give settlements in their favor, despite what he says are jurors' deep reservations about the redistribution of wealth. It is not that the jury is unsympathetic to the pain suffered by the plaintiff, he says, but rather that they are psychologically and politically uncomfortable with taking restitution from the defendant.[41] To counteract these reservations, Whitman turns to concepts from psychoanalysis, such as transference and projection, as ways to connect with the jury through subconscious means. Jurors, he writes, "can see the lawyer either as the unselfish father (or mother) of an intact family unit or as the detached, distant parent who doesn't really care about the family. If you want to win trials, it's best to appear as the caring and unselfish father (or mother) figure. Jurors, like all of us, have an unconscious need to please the caring parent."[42] For Whitman, narratology is thus important for attorneys to understand so that they may reconfigure the scripts that are preventing jurors from awarding in their favor. Offering a compelling narrative on behalf of the plaintiff must be more than a factual account supported by expert testimony, it must also meet unconscious psychological aspirations, such as pleasing a caring parent, and must do so in both verbal and nonverbal ways. Priming juror expectations during voir dire is another strategy advised by jury consultants attentive to the power of narrative. Reflecting on her experience helping with jury selection in defense cases that will hinge on understandings of civil disobedience, Lynne Williams describes using a special jury questionnaire that include questions such as "Do you think that the government lies to you?"[43] Even if the juror is not questioned about this topic again during voir dire, the establishment of the defense's narrative theme has begun. Bringing government deception to the fore of a juror's mind is also a way to preempt core principles that will be developed in the prosecution's narrative. The questionnaire, allowed by some judges on the grounds of expediency, serves as a way to alert jurors not only to the content of the competing narratives they will hear but to the form which the argument will take.

If both sides in criminal and civil cases have an interest in drawing attention to specific narrative constructions in order to curry favor and discredit the other side, is merely being in a courtroom enough to qualify as a juror education in narratology? From the perspective of turning doubt inward, it is not. The instrumental way in which attorneys and jury consultants lead juries to transfer, project, and question certainly begins a process of narrative awareness that may be advantageous for turning doubt inward, but it is not the same as a narrative awareness from the outset (one not connected to either side) about how narrative construction shapes a juror's interpretation of the facts. While an attorney's strategy always resolves any contradictions in the narratives in favor of her side, an orientation of doubt by each juror may reject the resolution and will instead consider how these contradictions relate to the function of the jury as an arbiter of the law.

Noting the challenge narratives present for the jury, Lisa Kern Griffin has suggested that there are ways to improve the jury's ability to assess doubt, particularly through jury instructions.[44] She calls for a reform of jury instructions to permit the judge to mention inadmissible evidence to the jury along with an explanation for why it is inadmissible. Such a process would, she argues, better neutralize the impact of the exclusion on deliberations later on, as would early instructions to the jury about the biasing effects of high-impact evidence such as gruesome photographs. Griffin writes, "A broader mandate for deliberation could thus mitigate some of the drawbacks of narrative constructs by exposing implicit processes to external critique and encouraging the formation of new commitments."[45] Her language of making the implicit process explicit is very much in the spirit of radical enfranchisement, but her reforms occur too late in the process. Radical enfranchisement requires a type of civic education before the trial (and apart from the power of judge in the courtroom) which introduces jurors to the idea of turning doubt inward as a way to counter the biases and shortcuts in thinking that take hold in juror decisions. In the context of learning prior to the courtroom, potential jurors have the opportunity to pose questions and concerns in a way that they are not able to do during the trial. They also have more time to contemplate what is truly being asked of them when they reconsider previously held beliefs and assumptions.

A Change in How We Hear Testimony

The case at the heart of the *Serial* podcast, hosted by Sarah Koenig in the fall of 2014, vividly illustrates the centrality of witness credibility to the workings of the trial.[46] The podcast focused on investigating the claim of innocence made by Adnan Syed, who is serving a life sentence for the 1999 killing of Hae Min Lee, his ex-girlfriend. Syed was convicted almost entirely on the testimony of Jay Wilds, his acquaintance, who says he assisted Syed in transporting and burying the body of Hae Min Lee. Through the course of the podcast, it becomes clear to the listener that the narratives Syed and Wilds tell about the night of the murder are riddled with inconsistencies; both must be lying in some capacity. It is, however, difficult to figure out why. Perhaps even more than in film, the podcast highlights how the listener, standing in for the jury, is constantly assessing credibility based on voice, accent, manner of speaking, and so on. I found myself having a strong negative reaction to the voice of the defense attorney, whose competence had been questioned earlier, and wondered how that would have swayed my evaluation of her argument were I on the jury. These judgments about the veracity and credibility of witnesses (and attorneys) are at the core of the jury's responsibility and a clear reason why it is human judgment, not technocratic formulas, that must be used to determine guilt. Yet it is precisely the foibles of human judgment—so subject to bias in ways that evade our attempts at detection—that easily take hold in the assessments of witnesses. Turning doubt inward during assessments of testimony is one means to scrutinize our intuitions about such judgments.

"Testimonial injustice" is Miranda Fricker's term for the situation where a witness suffers from a credibility deficit because of systematic prejudices about her intelligence or trustworthiness.[47] She identifies instances of it in everyday life and literature but notes that it is in a court of law that the consequences of testimonial injustice are translated to injustice full stop. Even more than material evidence, eyewitness accounts influence how a jury understands the case, with whom to have sympathy, and the motivations for a crime. If the testimonies of witnesses from certain demographic groups are repeatedly discounted, it is impossible for the checks built into the criminal justice system (such as the right to question one's accusers, to be presumed innocent, etc.) to effectively protect defendants or to ensure that the identity of a victim does not preclude a crime from getting punished. Fricker notes that an awareness of one's own identity in relation to the judgment one offers regarding another is part of the development of virtue necessary to counter testimonial injustice or to practice the type of doubt discussed in this chapter. She writes, "In testimonial exchanges, for hearers and speakers alike, no party is neutral; everybody has a race, everybody has a gender. What is needed on the part of the hearer in order to avert a testimonial injustice—and in order to serve his own epistemic interest in the truth—is a corrective, anti-prejudicial virtue that is reflexive in nature."[48] Doubt in relation to a juror's intuitions or initial judgments is one such reflexive move, and Fricker's suggestion is for an upward revision of credibility in order to achieve a level that would have obtained if not for the prejudice; she terms this a neutralization of prejudice. Before any neutralization can happen, one must first identify the likely presence of a bias, a task that the radically enfranchised juror will be prepared to do. While neutralization is part of the development of virtue and relies on a historical and sociological awareness of different types of prejudice, there is unfortunately no way to make this, or any other correction for bias, more precise.

In cases of police killings or "Stand Your Ground" assaults such as the case against George Zimmerman (for the killing of Trayvon Martin), the credibility of the defendant is intertwined with the perceptions of the (deceased) victim as threatening. When attorneys fail to mention the role racial stereotypes and unconscious bias may have played in the crime, the jury is, Cynthia Lee argues, much more likely to falsely believe that they are deliberating in a race-neutral way.[49] Instead, attitudes about race should be made salient during voir dire, opening statements, the testimony of laypeople about the racial attitudes of the defendant, and the practice of "race-switching" hypothetical scenarios (where the jury is asked to consider a scenario where the races of defendant and victim are altered).[50] Still, juror honesty about perceptions and vulnerabilities connected to the race of the defendant or victim may be hard to come by. Attorneys can set the tone for this type of candor, but since it is always calculated to achieve a particular type of sympathy, it is hard to tell jurors to take their advice to heart. In these cases doxa is made salient for the purpose of a particular end and not for the jury's own process of assessment. Take, for example, how Peter Joy advises a defense attorney in a case that hinged on a claim of self-defense on what to say to prospective jurors during a trial that took place in St. Louis shortly after Michael Brown was shot by a Ferguson police officer: "I'm a little afraid here. I'm scared. I walked by the police guarding the Justice Center, just as you did. Ferguson has been on the news nonstop, and it is hard not to think about it. Was anyone else a little fearful entering the Justice Center today?"[51]

Joy's advice brings the question of race to the fore during jury selection, but a juror engaged in the process of doubt would also be attuned to the narrative framing of the questions posed by the attorney and would question the assumptions embedded within. Joy's point is that a defense lawyer should aim to flush out the different types of implicit biases in the pool and then strategize about the most advantageous jury; a prosecutor should do the same. A juror attuned to the role of doubt prior to good judgment takes seriously the need to consider implicit associations with race and the police on both sides, but also the ways in which both narratives based on these associations are worthy of skepticism.

Judge Mark Bennett, a district judge in Iowa and one of the foremost voices in trying to address the problem of implicit bias in the courtroom, writes that current methods of judge-led voir dire and the scrutiny of juror selection in light of the *Batson* decision are exacerbating the problem of implicit bias.[52] To counter some of the adverse consequences of jurors who may be unaware of their explicit and implicit types of bias, Bennett makes the concept an explicit one in every trial in his courtroom by educating lawyers and jurors about implicit bias through a presentation.[53] In this way, he is priming jurors to do the work of turning doubt inward and questioning the assumptions and judgments they make during the trial. He also advocates for more questioning by lawyers, rather than judges, during voir dire. Controversially, Bennett reads a statement about implicit bias in his jury charge, including the following: "As we discussed in jury selection, growing scientific research indicates each one of us has 'implicit biases,' or hidden feelings, perceptions, fears and stereotypes in our subconscious. These hidden thoughts often impact how we remember what we see and hear and how we make important decisions. While it is difficult to control one's subconscious thoughts, being aware of these hidden biases can help counteract them."[54] The act of including such language in the jury charge is meant to address the central conundrum of bias in the reasonable doubt standard but is contentious for a variety of reasons. First, there is the danger, as evident in the aforementioned cases involving definitions of reasonable doubt, that more instruction from the judge will end up being the basis for an appeal because the excess verbiage compromised the meaning of reasonable doubt. Second, there is concern as to whether alerting people to implicit bias may in fact make those opinions more prominent in the decision-making process. Cynthia Lee has argued that experimental evidence refutes this implication; it is the ignorance of race as a factor that leads to more skewed outcomes. Yet the issue remains whether or not the call for more education about implicit bias will be able to mitigate the problems of racism in any significant way.

One of the most insidious aspects of implicit bias is its presence even in situations where people believe that they are attending to their own biases,

such as the alarm Judge Bennett felt when he displayed bias while participating in the Harvard online study. Telling jurors to pay attention to the idea
of bias without telling them what good judgment looks like seems ineffec-
tive. Given that studies continue to show that awareness of one's own implicit biases is not necessarily enough to change actions and outcomes, the
remedy of the sustained education of jurors on topics of implicit bias and
the impact of racist attitudes on punishment may arguably be severely limited and largely for the benefit of the scholars and reformers who insist on
prescribing it. But turning the concept of doubt inward, with the intellectual
and moral discomfort it causes, could slow down the process of judgment,
allowing the System 2 thinking described by Kahneman to take hold. Key
areas—presumption of innocence, the misdirection of narratives, and the
credibility deficit of certain witnesses—can be starting points for reflexive
thinking. To assume that doubt will be turned inward during the process
of a trial reflects a change in conventional juror expectations. In addition to
being thanked and applauded for one's dutiful service to the country, jurors
must also expect that they will find out what they do not know—about
themselves, their thinking, and the conditions of fair judgment—and that
this will be a disconcerting process. The goal of radical enfranchisement also
expands beyond offering judgment in the particular case, becoming instead
a tool to develop the practical wisdom to make judgments that incorporate
intuition without relying on them.

FOUR

Guilty, Not Guilty, Nullify: Nullification in an Age of Abolition

Verdicts are not "administered": they are found. And the findings in matters of "public importance" cannot yet be done by microchip. Men and women must consult their reason and their consciences, their precedents and their sense of who we are and who we have been.

—E. P. Thompson, *Writing by Candlelight*

Radical enfranchisement as a type of citizenship is brought into sharpest relief with the issue of nullification, the secret power held by jurors to find a defendant not guilty despite an assessment of the evidence that would suggest otherwise. Debates over this power of the jury take on a tenor distinct from other issues raised here because of what critics see as the proximity between jury nullification and an undermining of the rule of law in a way that destabilizes democracy altogether. Fears of mob rule, that primal force of democracy, are also activated through discussions of nullification, especially in relation to cases both of lynching in the South, where juries seemed to use their power of nullification to acquit white defendants, and the contemporary iteration of acquittals in police brutality cases. Skeptics on both the right and the left thus have reasons for wanting to minimize the salience of nullification. Yet, it is precisely because of its potent impact that education about nullification and its deployment are necessary. The qualities of citizenship that constitute radical enfranchisement, including an adversarial relationship between judge and jury, an understanding of the task of justice as greater than an assessment of evidence, and an awareness of the responsibilities of self-scrutiny that come with all verdicts have a heightened urgency with the issue of nullification.

While arguments for greater awareness about nullification and the critical role it plays within the legal system have long existed, its relationship to contemporary movements for racial justice, particularly the Movement for Black Lives, has been underdeveloped. One reason for this is that the movement grew out of a desire for greater accountability for police violence against African-Americans, a pattern that had been largely ignored within the public consciousness and also unpunished within the criminal justice system. We can recall the Rodney King trial of 1992, where four white Los Angeles Police Department officers were acquitted of assault and of unlawful use of force despite video footage of the incident that showed King being brutally beaten. It is striking how similar the narratives of that trial are to contemporary trials where officers are acquitted and jurors recount that race did not play a role in their deliberations.[1] The jurors often say that it was their finding that the officers were following standard procedure given the dangers they faced. In light of these concerns, it is no wonder that nullification does not emerge as a critical strategy for movements for racial justice. Yet, examining the argument for nullification, the need for greater education about its role, and the force of the jury allows for the development of the radically enfranchised citizen in ways that would enhance movements calling for dramatic changes within the criminal justice system. The education involved in radical enfranchisement also involves considering alternatives to incarceration for punishment that is consistent with democratic aspirations for all citizens, even those who have been convicted of a felony. The potential juror who maintains consistent responsibility for decisions about punishment made in her name as a citizen will be better poised to thoughtfully exercise her rights in the courtroom as a juror.

The demands listed as part of the Movement for Black Lives include, but are not limited to, (1) an end to capital punishment, (2) an end to the use of criminal history to determine eligibility for housing, education, and voting, (3) the demilitarization of law enforcement, and (4) an end to prison, jails, and detention centers as we know them, including an end to solitary confinement. The platform is extensive but nowhere are juries or the centrality of jury service mentioned, despite an interest in institutional reforms, perhaps because of the small number of cases. Yet, an analysis of the significance of jury nullification and the conditions for its use can bolster not only the aims of the movement but also integrate the individual and institutional transformations necessary. Considering the basis for nullification sharpens what citizens are called to do in the pursuit of justice and provides a way to reconcile two levels of concern that often seem at odds: (1) systemic patterns of racial injustice and (2) the need for discretion in individual cases. There is also the challenge of protecting the rights of the defendant in all cases, even those whose actions are the result of racism. I will argue that the qualities of radical enfranchisement manifested in education about nullification and a new three-option verdict (guilty, not guilty, nullify) can serve to enhance the transformative vision of racial justice put forth by the Movement for Black Lives. These qualities are grounded in republican theories of participation but emphasize a confrontational approach to elite leadership and the law.

Enshrined in the tradition of common law, nullification is a power, though not a right, that allows jurors to be the final decision-makers in a trial, carrying more authority than the judge. Consistent with the presumption of innocence in an adversarial system, the judge must ensure that a guilty verdict is not reached by a jury through erroneous means or a corrupt process, but the not guilty verdict cannot be overturned through the same process of scrutiny. The state holds the burden of proof and must prove beyond a reasonable doubt that the defendant committed the crime; the jury is not at liberty to adjust this extremely high standard for guilt.[2] However, when the jury offers a verdict of not guilty, the judge cannot overturn it, even if she disagrees about whether the burden of proof was met. When a not guilty verdict seems to be inconsistent with the evidence in a case or the conventional understanding of the law, the court must respect the decision. Such a not guilty decision may be (1) predicated on the law itself being unjust and not worthy of enforcement or (2) based on the particular circumstances of the defendant that make leniency a salient concern. Both outcomes could be considered acts of jury nullification and are unusual because in forty-eight states, jurors are not told of their power; and they typically assume the conventional interpretation of juror responsibility that can be summarized as "jurors decide on the facts and judges decide on the law." For a jury to decide on the legitimacy of the law in a particular case is, to many, an overreach of its task.

The Constitution makes no mention of nullification in part because it was a widely accepted tradition in the Anglo-American system, particularly as embodied in *Bushel*, the famous seventeenth-century case involving the William Penn trial. The jury was punished for its not guilty finding: food was withheld from the jury with the hope that jurors would change their minds; later a fine was imposed on them. A member of the jury contested the punishment and the higher court found that a jury could not be punished on account of the verdict it returned, even when court officials disagreed.[3] The decision of jurors to engage in an act of nullification is the crucible for testing the skills connected to enfranchisement that I have described in earlier chapters.

While jury nullification is vulnerable to the harshest type of criticism, including that it introduces instability, bias, and corruption into a legal system whose integrity depends on the disavowal of these concepts, it is a powerful response to systemic deficits that would not otherwise be addressed. Thus, the argument presented here has two prongs: the first is that a transformation in thinking about jury service through the lens of radical enfranchisement—particularly the principles of a productive adversarial relationship between the judge and jury, the benefits of the agonistic encounter of mass and elite in the courtroom, and the implications of sovereign decision-making by the jury—should change the way the act of nullification is understood. Instead of being maintained as a fiercely guarded secret, nullification should widely be known as an important deployment of the power of laypeople in democracy. Second, the chapter will explore, as a thought experiment, what might happen if the American criminal justice system employed a three-option verdict: guilty, not guilty, nullify.

The argument articulated here for the role and predisposition of the jury is more consistent with Francis Lieber, the nineteenth-century German-American law professor, than with the conventional interpretation of juries in the work of Alexis de Tocqueville.[4] Tocqueville's assessment of jurors, much like his assessment of the civic role of women, is hobbled by his refusal to grant them a status of maturity, an issue which is also at the crux of a transformed vision of racial justice that includes greater community control of political, economic, and legal outcomes. For Tocqueville, both jurors and women are promising students of democracy but cannot be trusted with the most complex types of decisions, even though their involvement would help mitigate some of the greatest weaknesses of democracy, including the tyranny of the majority and the deadening effects of rule by bureaucracy. Rather than the "free school" metaphor favored by Tocqueville that highlights juries as inchoate incubators of civic sensibilities and respect for the majesty of the law, Lieber presents the value of a much higher degree of ambivalence between judges and juries, a distinctive component of an orientation of radical enfranchisement. While Tocqueville celebrates hierarchical respect for the legal profession that emerges after jury service, Lieber stresses what jurors themselves bring to the process of legal judgment. It is precisely because the legal profession has become a closed caste that there is a heightened need for a check by outsiders before the spark of revolution. The discretion the jury exercises when it chooses to nullify can be seen as a pointed moment of such a check on the executive or otherwise closed caste that consistently dominates legal and political decision-making. The jury serves as watchdog for officials and forces a break in the momentum accrued by government insiders and repeat players to bend the law to their will.[5] In light of the goals of the Movement for Black Lives, an adversarial relationship between the jury and other officers of the court can be seen as an extension of the adversarial orientation that has been necessary to bring issues of police brutality and systemic racism to the fore. It is also consistent with the questioning of legal expertise and the administration of justice that the movement brings up.

The concept that tension between elite and nonelite is desirable is a core concept within the tradition of republicanism given contemporary voice by Philip Pettit and John McCormick.[6] For Pettit, the Italian republican tradition, as distinct from the Rousseauian one, is marked by an understanding of freedom as nondomination, and he marks the threats to such freedom as stemming from two primary sources: the state and the people. While a despotic government leads to domination in the lives of citizens, so can decisions made by the people who purport to speak in one voice. Good governance and the liberty it ensures require constant vigilance, even when such governance is being conducted democratically.[7] To that end, a mixed constitution with opportunities for checks and balances, including the involvement of nonelites, is necessary. Pettit also asserts the need for a resistive culture where citizens cultivate "contestatory virtue" and are "committed to establishing an undominating government in their country."[8] Radically enfranchised jurors could contribute to such a resistive culture.

McCormick, drawing on Machiavelli's republican analysis, emphasizes the necessity of formal institutional spaces for the *grandi* and the *populi* to voice their differing concerns. Without formal spaces, there will be not only more opportunities for the abuse of power by the few, the possibilities of revolution also increase. Machiavelli's key insight, then, is that the elite should fear the retribution of the many, and that formal spaces for such contestations of power are necessary for the republic. When considering the power of the masses, McCormick writes, "Their retribution must be decided collectively through formalized procedures, and not exacted though mob violence; and certainly not through unilateral action by a would-be prince."[9] In thinking about the contemporary application of Machiavelli's insight, McCormick imagines a modern People's Tribunate of fifty-one nonelite citizens *chosen by lot* as a way to demonstrate what a formalized check on elite rule might look like.[10] McCormick suggests that the tribunate have veto power over legislation, an executive order, and a Supreme Court decision (exactly one each) in order to prevent oligarchic rule. His heuristic functions as a challenge for thinking about modern-day reforms rather than a blueprint for institutional design, but one veto (or even the threat of veto) in each of those domains would not change political culture in the way that he hopes.[11] Nullification, however, can chip away at institutional and substantive encroachment by elite interests in the public sphere through iterative engagement with the law. The American jury should be seen in a way consistent with Machiavelli's insights, as a formalized check on elite rule that includes, in extraordinary cases, a decision on the legitimacy of the law. Consistent with this line of republican thought, the argument for the radical enfranchisement of jurors turns on the necessity of explicit power contestation within the legal and political system, not on the assumption that collective decisions are more accurate.

While arguments for the jury's power to nullify based in Lieber and Machiavelli foreground the relational value of a jury in tension with the judge, Mortimer Kadish and Sanford Kadish offer a persuasive reading of the *legitimate interposition* of the jury grounded in Anglo-American legal thought, a critical procedural role that only jurors can play, and one that is consistent with their decision-making sovereignty in the courtroom. Kadish and Kadish write:

> Actions are legitimated for a role agent insofar as the role justifies an argu-
> ment to appropriateness for the action. When a legal system presents an
> official with the liberty to depart from a rule that might work against his
> achieving the ends of his role, it legitimates his departure from the rule; that
> is, it legitimates the interposition between the rule and his action of his own
> judgment that departure from the rule best serves the prescribed end.[12]

In their formulation, it is the end of a just verdict that is of ultimate importance; the rules that direct the jury toward these ends may or may not be helpful to achieving them, and the jury, in certain cases, may put itself between the rule and the desired end by committing an act that contravenes the rule. Kadish and Kadish emphasize that a consideration of a wide array of options for action is open to jurors from the *very beginning* of deliberation, not only when they may have "damn good reasons" for breaking with convention.[13] By foregrounding the legitimacy of the range of actions that a jury can take, they are dismissing claims that jury action is best understood as consistent with the distinction between rules (always binding) and principles (open to context and contingency), a typology offered by Ronald Dworkin.[14] Kadish and Kadish refuse to place the weight of justification of the power of the jury in the parsing of concepts. They see no value to seeking greater precision about when and how a jury may legitimately "depart" from the rules (in a manner that evokes arguments given for protests against police brutality today); such precision can never be found, but an alternative exists in the incorporation of such ambiguity into the essence of the jury as the bridge between legal and political life. Democracy depends on a laboratory for the exploration of checks to elite power, legal convention, and retributive justice—the power of juries to nullify is essential for this purpose.

While Kadish and Kadish do not think it is possible or desirable to enumerate the criteria for legitimate rule departures (as this would be in conflict with the concept of legitimate interposition), they maintain that departures that are not consistent with the accepted ends of the function of juries are not legitimate. Bribery, vindictiveness, or loyalty to the defendant, to name just a few, are not consistent with the ends of jury service within the criminal justice system and thus not acceptable actions even when they are interventions counter to the law. In response to the common criticism that nullification will be misused by narrow-minded, prejudicial jurors, Kadish and Kadish respond, "Any liberty may be misused. But if our interpretation is right, the law has chosen to take that chance in the case of the jury."[15] I take their defense of the acquittal in the lynching case as ripe for further elaboration, such as with the demands of self-scrutiny described previously. Not all nullifying juries have done the internal work required to legitimate such a verdict; radical enfranchisement entails understanding the context for discretion. The jury as a whole, as well as individual jurors, must not only draw a superficial connection between the reasons given for the decision and the ends of their role, but they must subject themselves to an even higher level of scrutiny given the realities of unconscious bias (a phenomenon not widely discussed when Kadish and Kadish were writing). The process of cognitive and ethical investigation that is constitutive of radical enfranchisement thus places additional demands on the jury. Radical enfranchisement, as an ambitious way of thinking about jury service, is built upon a more comprehensive version of the decision-making process and is thus able to better respond to concerns about the misuse of nullification. Still, no theory can entirely separate nullification as a legitimate check on the state versus nullification as a tool of the powerful, just as no theory of democracy can excise its potential for demagoguery.

Legitimate interposition in the service of radical enfranchisement intersects with arguments about the role of mercy within the criminal justice system, another concept that is part of the civic education necessary for jury service. Radical enfranchisement does not single mercy out as an isolated ideal for jurors to consider, but it is captured within the function of the jury that goes beyond fact-finding to offer a verdict consistent with their understanding of what justice demands in a particular case. Debates about mercy in public life share with critics of nullification a concern that justice is being thwarted. I am persuaded by the argument made by Alex Tuckness and John Parrish that mercy is not the opposite of justice but is in fact the opposite of cruelty, and thus a fitting area of jurisdiction for a group made up of the defendant's peers. Tuckness and Parrish have also argued that mercy itself has become a hobbled concept in contemporary life because of the admixture of metaphors on which it depends, including that of "the lenient judge, the forgiving creditor, the merciful benefactor, or the loving parent" and the theological foundations which continue to inform them.[16] None of these are collective bodies, and the metaphors reveal that the personalization of power within a highly unequal relationship has come to define the term. Mercy in a different context, one where it is offered by a group of peers, thereby demands a new, as yet undiscovered metaphor. Jury nullification upends long-standing tropes with its intervention by a collective body, but it does not conform to the hopes for transparency and accountability that Tuckness and Parrish proffer to assuage concerns about the just use of discretion. Even in the thought experiment described below, juries will not be expected to explain why they nullified nor the role mercy played in that decision. However, the naming of a nullification verdict as distinct from a not guilty one follows the logic they offer in their argument for the more frequent use of mercy in public discussion.

The Status of Nullification in the Courts

Examining the assumptions about jurors that undergird debates on nullification sharpens what is at stake in different conceptions of citizenship that are activated through jury service. Three legal cases are particularly important in thinking both about the current legitimacy of jury nullification in the US and the related issue of whether a jury should ever be notified of the option to nullify; they also reveal how jurors are often not seen to be capable of radical enfranchisement. In the case of US v. Dougherty (1972), the District of Columbia appeals court considered whether the jury that decided the case of the D. C. 9 (charged with breaking and entering Dow Chemical Company to protest against its manufacturing involvement in the Vietnam War) should have been alerted of its option to nullify. The defense suggested that the legality of the war in Southeast Asia should be considered when determining the culpability of the D. C. 9. After conviction for unlawful entry, the defense appealed, suggesting that the judge should have notified the jury of their right to nullify.[17] They lost the appeal.[18] In writing for the majority, Justice Leventhal articulated the delicate balance that still dominates thinking about jury nullification when he warned that an overt instruction to the jury that they are to consider the law as well as the facts of the case (similar to language used in courts in Maryland, Indiana, and, as of 2011, New Hampshire) will lead to chaos in the verdicts.[19] He suggested that jurors would not be able to successfully complete the tasks of assessing evidence and determining guilt beyond a reasonable doubt with the distraction of this other command. Leventhal also considered notification about the nullification option to be an undue burden on jurors to think like legislators and consider the many implications of their actions. As part of another line of thinking, he used the analogy of speeding to make his point about the danger of latitude, as fostered by notifying the jury of the power to nullify, and wrote, "We know that a posted limit of 60 m.p.h. produces factual speeds 10 or even 15 miles greater, with an understanding all around that some 'tolerance' is acceptable to the authorities, assuming conditions warrant. But can it be supposed that the speeds would stay substantially the same if the speed limit were put: Drive as fast as you think appropriate, without the posted limit as an anchor, a point of departure?"[20] This analogy is erroneous in that jury nullification, as it stands now, is essentially a one-off decision not meant to set precedent in any formal way, and unlikely to change the actions of others. While the analogy is effective in highlighting the human tendency to exceed existing boundaries, nullification is not tied to the safety of large numbers of people and the considered contestation of boundaries is part of the jury's role within the closed caste of legal and state power. Leventhal assumes that in exceptional cases the jury will try to exceed the boundaries of the instruction and will somehow *know* how to act on behalf of the conscience of its members, yet there is no acknowledgment of the skills that might be required to reach such a decision.

Leventhal's orientation reveals the disjuncture between conventional understandings of jury competence and the practice of radical enfranchisement. The language of the majority opinion suggests that the average juror should focus only on the task of judging the facts of the case, implying that she will never be able to develop the maturity to consider an always-live alternative of nullification. Instead, Leventhal accepts the possibility that a few jurors may, based on prior knowledge, be aware of the power of nullification or will be moved spontaneously to consider it. His position neither privileges the awareness of nullification in all jurors nor thinks about the trial as a process for developing the skills necessary to enact nullification in a thoughtful manner. The majority decision captures the sentiment, consistent with the received view, that sees the court as trusted with saving jurors from themselves.

In the minority decision, Justice Bazelon takes umbrage at Leventhal's depiction of the logic of nullification. Bazelon does not think that the *spontaneous* movement of the highly principled jury to nullify would be less biased than the informed jury who had known about the concept beforehand. He writes, "It seems substantially more plausible to me to assume that the very opposite is true. The juror motivated by prejudice seems to me more likely to make spontaneous use of the power to nullify, and more likely to disregard the judge's exposition of the normally controlling legal standards. The conscientious juror, who could make a careful effort to consider the blameworthiness of the defendant's action in light of prevailing community values, is the one most likely to obey the judge's admonition that the jury enforce strict principles of law."[21] His invocation of the predisposition of the conscientious juror is particularly astute in that it captures the possibility that the importance of jury nullification necessitates that *all* jurors think about it thoughtfully, with a full understanding of its value and limitations. Secrecy about the existence of the nullification option makes its application more dependent on those within the jury who are the most vocal and can persuade others of its validity. These "triggers" may not be the best people to lead the discussion, but they obtain that role by default.

The question of whether jury nullification should be understood as a "right" was raised in the case of *US v. Thomas* (1997), the precedent that guides much of courtroom behavior on the topic today.[22] Compared to *US v. Dougherty*, this case exhibited greater hostility toward the idea of jury nullification and created a conundrum regarding how a juror could be cognizant of the possibility of nullification (and vocal about this) and, at the same time, not be seen in "purposeful disregard of the law," a punishable offense.[23] The case involved a district court judge who removed Juror #5 because other jurors had found him to be disruptive. During the jury's deliberation Juror #5 had allegedly mentioned that he found the law in question to be lacking merit and that he felt racial solidarity with the defendant. When this was reported to the judge and verified, he was dismissed. The appeals court found that the lower court had wrongly dismissed the juror because it was not clear that a desire for nullification was motivating his statements; he could, in fact, have been committed to acquittal on evidentiary grounds.

While this ruling bypasses the question of what would have happened had Juror #5 been making a subtle case for nullification alongside a claim based on reasonable doubt (two perspectives easily harmonized), the court offered its narrow interpretation of the historical right to nullify in starker terms than ever before. They wrote, "We categorically reject the idea that, in a society committed to the rule of law, jury nullification is desirable or that courts may permit it to occur when it is within their authority to prevent. Accordingly, we conclude that a juror who intends to nullify the applicable law is no less subject to dismissal than is a juror who disregards the court's instructions due to an event or relationship that renders him biased or otherwise unable to render a fair and impartial verdict."[24] Such language sets in motion a court that is obligated to quell even the initial stirrings of nullification. Moreover, the court wrote, "The power of juries to 'nullify' or exercise a power of lenity is just that—a power; it is by no means a right or something that a judge should encourage or permit if it is within his authority to prevent." Radical enfranchisement captures this tension between right and power as described in the opinion. Enfranchisement in the jury context, as with voting, is a right ensured by the state and comes with a minimal set of requirements. To understand its radical capacities is to think about it as a power to be cultivated under particular conditions with a more developed set of civic and individual skills. By focusing on the evidentiary question and vacating the lower court's ruling, the decision in US v. Thomas also seems to suggest that the hung jury is the closest a jury should come to nullification. If Juror #5 was not convinced by the evidence and had voted to acquit and this resulted in a hung jury, the outcome could be seen as a legally acceptable way to exercise one's conscience in the jury process. As evident in these two influential precedents, jury nullification exists in uneasy tension with the courts: it is not prohibited and is certainly in line with the role accorded to juries in the common law system, but the precedents have made it clear that jury nullification should not be publicized or celebrated.

Nonetheless, the appellate decision in US v. Spock (1969), with its ruling on special verdicts, buffers the legitimacy of nullification in another way and reveals how much the radical enfranchisement of the jury is one that turns on the *tone* in which jury power is described: the tone of the judge, the tone of citizenship in anticipation of jury cases, and the tone of deliberations. In the 1969 case Dr. Benjamin Spock and three others had been found guilty of aiding and abetting the evasion of the draft. Their defense had rested on First Amendment protections of free speech, but they were found guilty by a Boston jury who had been told by the judge that the case was "not trying the legality, morality or constitutionality of the war in Vietnam, or the rights of a citizen to protest," a warning that jettisoned any opening for nullification.[25] The First Circuit vacated the ruling in part because of the list of factual questions (a special verdict) given to the jury by the judge. While special verdicts are common in civil cases, the court argued that they were impermissible in criminal cases because they increased the judge's ability to influence a guilty verdict through the suggestion that factual findings should lead to an overall finding of guilt.[26] The decision reads, "There is no easier way to reach, and perhaps force, a verdict of guilty than to approach it step by step. A juror, wishing to acquit, may be formally catechized. By a progression of questions each of which seems to require an answer unfavorable to the defendant, a reluctant juror may be led to vote for a conviction which, in the large, he would have resisted."[27] Such a ruling on special verdicts in criminal trials also suggests that a finding of guilt by the jury is more than an agreed-upon tally of guilty actions. The jury is always able to assert a verdict of not guilty, even if they might have answered yes to a litany of questions about the defendant's culpability. The court thus preserves a space between not only what an outside observer or legal expert may consider grounds for a guilty verdict and what the jury is able to do, but also between the "technical requirements" of guilt (a consideration of the burden of proof for each charge) and the proclamation of a guilty verdict. The decision in *US v. Spock* makes it clear that courts may be more willing to limit the coercive influence of a judge than actively highlight the power of a jury to nullify, even if both orientations ultimately limn the same concept of jury independence.

The argument for radical enfranchisement, particularly the skills of greater accuracy and impartiality in adjudicating the evidence and greater awareness of the political dimensions of the jury's power to block punishment by the state, is aligned with the findings in the Spock case about the coercive nature of special verdicts and the implication that a judge can lead a jury to a guilty verdict through a series of questions about the facts. Yet there may be another way to understand the issue. What if special verdicts were, in fact, better able to communicate the gravity of the guilty verdict as separate from a finding of the facts? The gravity of a judge's charge and the desire to have performed competently as a jury may be more pronounced for jurors during deliberation than their understanding of the contingency of the power to punish. A special verdict could arguably remind radically enfranchised jurors of their additional task of affirming punishment just when it is most important, that is, after they have deliberated on the details of the case and are in a position to question what justice means in this case.[28] Still, opening up the use of special verdicts may backfire in just the ways the justices in the Spock case feared if the jurors do not already have a sense of the extent of their power (and the ways it could be misused).[29]

In the normative ideal, when the radically enfranchised jury is deliberating a case, jurors should first weigh the evidence and decide whether the prosecution has met the burden of proof, taking into account the mistakes and misperceptions discussed earlier, and then they should consider whether a guilty verdict and the retributive sentence that will follow is consistent with their understanding of justice in the case. At this juncture, the radically enfranchised juror may want to consider whether or not there are values beyond fidelity to the standard of evidence that are prominent in their understanding of justice in a particular case. For example, the potential relevance of questions of mercy, fairness, the lack of integrity of the prosecution, and the intended effects of the law may become central to jurors. Ideally, greater public discussion around nullification will make each of these dimensions more familiar to jurors prior to their service; it will include debate on whether nullification may be the correct verdict. Throughout this process, jurors should have a heightened sense of their role as the defendant's peers in relation to the state, as the only ones in the trial who have the power to slow down the levers of violence enacted on the defendant.

The Benefits of the Three-Option Verdict

In conversation with others who want a more prominent role for jury nullification, I find affinities with Nancy Marder, Clay Conrad, Jeffery Abramson, and David Brody who have argued for the increasing prominence of nullification, the notification of it to juries, and its legislative importance.[30] The jury finding of a verdict of not guilty despite substantial evidence serves as a conduit between legal and political life, providing distinctive benefits to both that correct for systemic deficits.[31] In this way, it is similar to Michael Hall's proposal for a verdict of "Guilty but Civilly Disobedient (GBCD)" as a way for civil disobedience to "retain a sufficiently distinct moral status such that society as a whole respects its place in the political order. If civil disobedience loses its clarity, if the sharp edges demarking the firebreak deteriorate, civil disobedience fails in its role, loses its force, and erodes the rule of law."[32] With nullification, there is even greater secrecy and ambiguity around its proper place in the legal system. A formalization of its role with a "nullify" option would serve a pedagogic function for the public and potential jurors while holding up other pillars of the criminal process. What might happen if instead of the guilty/not guilty options the jury currently has, it were presented with a three-option verdict—guilty, not guilty, nullify? The hypothetical scenario of a three-option verdict would end the secrecy around nullification because it is evident for all to see, separate of a judge's discretion in the jury charge. It would also warrant a more prominent place for discussions of nullification within civic education, including public feedback following a nullification verdict. Ending the secrecy around nullification is not only a commitment to educating citizens about their powers as jurors in the abstract, it should also be a conversation about the ways such powers have been used and abused.

The charge to the jury with a three-option verdict might follow the one offered by David Brody:

> While it is proper and advisable for you to follow the law as I give it, you are not required to do so. You must, however, keep in mind that we are a nation governed by laws. Refusal to follow the court's instructions as to the elements of the crime(s) charged should occur only in an extraordinary case. Unless finding the defendant guilty is repugnant to your sense of justice, you should follow the instruction on the law as given to you by the court. You must also keep in mind that you may not find the defendant guilty unless the State has established guilt beyond a reasonable doubt as it was defined previously in these instructions.

The potency of nullification comes in the intersection of politics and the law, and the first benefit of a "nullify" option, providing feedback to the prosecutor, would be to draw attention to the discretion and accountability of the state in its role of bringing charges against its citizens.[33] As a type of information for the prosecutor's office, a jury's decision to nullify a charge could be a powerful counterweight to the tremendous discretion the prosecutor has in determining which charges to bring.[34] Moreover, there is great potential for prosecutorial bullying of the defendant in the hope of achieving a plea bargain, and it is difficult to critique such actions from the outside. While plea-bargained cases would never get to a jury, the actions of a jury in similar cases could be informative and serve as a calibrating measure for overzealous prosecutions. Nullification by the jury would indicate that the case was a misguided effort by the state and one that the defendant's peers cannot endorse.

The inclusion of laypeople in the decision to nullify is the source of its normative power and could arguably be a source of confidence in its outcome. Drawing on a historical case, Josiah Ober writes on the highly adaptive Athenian model of the incorporation of laypeople in the legal process.[35] Ober presents a middle path between the deliberation of citizens (and the subsequent tallying of preferences) and the role of expertise in what he calls REA, Relevant Expertise Aggregation.[36] In the model of REA, after a round of initial deliberation and voting establishes the relevant criterion for thinking about a particular issue, an administrative council would solicit experts on each criterion and record their opinions. These perspectives would then be circulated to the larger group, who would make the final decision. Such a process still privileges the wisdom of the group in making the tradeoffs between different criteria as well as in choosing which expert opinions to incorporate and which to ignore. While Ober posits the REA approach as a superior way to conduct democratic politics, it is very similar to what already happens in the jury process. The criteria for a fair trial are predetermined and a variety of relevant experts, including lawyers on both sides, the judge, and expert witnesses, present information to a group of laypeople who have the ultimate decision-making authority. Ober's argument suggests that the jury system we have may, in fact, be an optimal way of combining expert knowledge and the intuitive and deliberative value of discussion among nonexperts.[37]

Ober has also argued that previous upheaval and demands for land restitution in the fifth century led the Athenian elite to be keenly aware of the interdependent nature of its relationship to the populace.[38] All the stability, wealth, and cultural prominence of democratic life could be eroded if the needs and perspectives of the nonelite were ignored. A critical space to counteract such a possibility was in the Assembly where the masses knew that they had the power to scorn or dispossess the wealthy and the wealthy, in turn, knew that they needed to take (rhetorically and substantively) the concerns of the masses into consideration. There are ways in which the argument for a three-option verdict is a similarly institutional mechanism for nonelites to impact the law and to insure that the evolving conversation on justice and the law involves such voices. To draw a further (Machiavellian) parallel to Ober, jury nullification could be seen as a release valve for calcified resentments that could very well lead to a disregard for the law altogether. Yet, I place the emphasis on the unexpectedness of jury nullification rather than on the routinization of an ideology that includes both mass and elite. By unexpectedness, I mean that the verdict of "nullify" is not a means to placate a populace but rather to draw attention to an urgent issue or an exceptional case deserving of leniency. Making nullification routine is a fear harbored by its opponents, but radical enfranchisement demands that it be understood as the exceptional moment, only undertaken after great consideration.

The first benefit of a nullification option—a direct reaction to the prosecutorial strategy of the state—is a dynamic that is already at play according to Paul Butler, one the most vocal proponents of nullification in the popular media.[39] In scholarly articles and newspaper editorials, he has argued that jurors should use the right of nullification to remedy some of the systematic biases against African-Americans that occur in the legal system as the result of punitive sentencing policies in drug cases. He argues that black jurors should come into nonviolent drug cases prepared to issue a not-guilty verdict but not to do so in cases where there are children involved. In cases of murder, rape, robbery, theft, public corruption, corporate fraud, any other crime of violence, or any crime that has a victim, Butler calls for a conventional understanding of the burden of proof. In addition to such jury action as a method of communication with the prosecution, Butler is also drawing attention to the impact of incarceration for nonviolent drug crimes on the defendant's community, a consideration that follows from the hope that jurors will be peers of the defendant and able to recognize collective concerns and the possibility of alternatives to incarceration.

A three-option verdict would be an expansion of Butler's hopes for how African-Americans, and other concerned citizens, should think about the adjudication of drug crimes.[40] A three-option verdict would force a consideration of a variety of cases, as well as explicit public reflection on cases that end with a nullification verdict. The not guilty verdicts that have been frequent in police violence cases that have video evidence demonstrate how the refusal to punish can serve a variety of political ends. Furthermore, they also show how too much prosecutorial responsiveness to jury action (a moratorium on prosecuting police officers, for example) may be out of sync with other democratic needs. Having an option to nullify would, however, make it more clear whether the jury was persuaded by the evidence or by another rationale, an insight that could give clues as to how police violence cases are adjudicated or the impact of racial bias on the assessments of the defendants and victim.

The second benefit of a three-option verdict is found in the bridge it provides between the legal and political worlds, since a verdict of nullification can serve as a source of information for lawmakers about the justness, utility, and applicability of a law. The exercise of the nullification option would provide an alternate source of information to voters (who may have been jurors themselves) and lawmakers about the application and the interpretation of laws. The outcome of a hung jury cannot be interpreted as commentary on the legislation (and is declared a mistrial and subject to further action), and the current format of a simple verdict of not guilty from a jury is ambiguous as well, because such a verdict could be decided on the evidence and not tied to nullification. With such murky indicators, observers are left to string together patterns, such as acquittals in marijuana or "three strikes" cases, in order to decipher the perspective of the jury.[41] The actions of a jury in such cases already serve as harbingers of what law in the future could look like, but this function becomes more explicit through a three-option verdict.[42] While protests, social movements, referenda, and lobbying efforts all work to change legislation, the three-option scenario provides another way to formalize the process, and thus formalize another dimension of agonistic debate, in the manner of the Machiavellian Tribunate and of the Athenenian model of mass and elite communication as described by Ober.

Understanding juror action through a three-option verdict also provides a framework for the juror to keep in mind both the systemic failures of the criminal justice system and the ideal that each defendant be treated as an individual. This simultaneous consideration may be one of the most important skills of radical enfranchisement, and one that could be incorporated more fully into contemporary social movements for racial justice. The way systemic racism pervades every aspect of the criminal justice system must be taken into account during a trial, but this does not mean that appropriate punishment is either impossible or peripheral to the concern of citizens who are committed to more revolutionary causes. Expanding alternatives to incarceration, including via mechanisms of restorative justice, requires sustained thinking about the particular circumstances of punishment, even for those who ultimately want prison abolition.

A vision of radically enfranchised democratic citizenship within the criminal justice system builds on the work of scholars who have considered how blameworthiness should be calculated, given the varied life circumstances of defendants. R. A. Duff draws attention to conditions where the defendant has been excluded from political life, has no political voice, is deprived of material and economic benefits, and is denied "by the state and her fellow citizens the respect and concern due to her as a citizen."[43] The political, economic, and psychological valences of this list resonate with the scope of racial injustice at the crux of the Movement for Black Lives; both accounts draw attention to the moral status of society that must also be under scrutiny when a defendant is charged with a crime or, in the case of police violence, when the use of force by law enforcement is questioned. One approach to blameworthiness suggests that victims of these kinds of injustices cannot be legitimately tried and punished by the criminal justice system. The incentives to commit or not commit a crime have been distorted to such an extent that punishment cannot be justified. A biased and unreflective jury is also likely to replicate the lack of respect and concern demonstrated by society at large. A dismantling of the institutions and attitudes that perpetuate injustice on a mass scale thus becomes paramount with individual cases receding as objects of analysis. Yet, while the goal of abolishing prisons may serve as the political lodestar, an alternative approach is to use the jury to reduce the number of crimes for which prison is an appropriate outcome. Radically enfranchised jurors work to exercise power at the point when they most have it: the verdict. Considering the jury's power to nullify is a return to highlighting individual cases while also taking into account the structural problems of the legal code or its enforcement. Thus what nullification can offer the vision of political action described by the Movement for Black Lives is a practice of citizenship that acknowledges the pervasive nature of racial injustice, but also includes developing the skills of judgment in the consideration of individual cases. Justice on a societal scale may only come with an end to prisons as we known them, but there are civic skills that can be developed through the transition and then activated to sustain democratic institutions consistent with the new reality.

FIVE

Radical Enfranchisement in the Jury Room

All punishments that exceed what is necessary to preserve this bond are unjust by their very nature. One must be aware of attaching the idea of something real to this word "justice," as though it were a physical force or a being that actually exists. It is simply a human manner of conceiving things, a manner that has an infinite influence on the happiness of everybody.

—Cesare Beccaria, *On Crimes and Punishments*

In the current moment the vast majority of cases will never go to trial, fewer and fewer citizens will ever serve on a jury, and judges describe what it feels like to sit on the bench for years without ever overseeing a jury trial.[1] What, then, is the point of an orientation of radical enfranchisement grounded in the jury system? Such an orientation has the power to revitalize involvement in questions of punishment and civic responsibility in legal and political life, but it requires three distinct stages of development. An orientation of radical enfranchisement emerges from (1) the civic education that must occur prior to jury service, (2) the learning that is scaffolded by the conventions of the trial, and (3) the collective reflection on jury verdicts that should occur after the fact in a way that incorporates them into the culture of citizenship. Juries and the process of deliberation that occur within them represent moments of great contingency and possibility, a fact often forgotten when only the verdict is remembered. Greater attention to the process of jury service and the political perspectives that emerged during the trial and deliberation but were later obscured is the final dimension of radical enfranchisement. To that end, this chapter will consider several notable jury trials and the key moments that revealed the desire of jurors for a more expansive understanding of their power, as well as moments that showed how jurors may be unsure of how to use this power if they have not developed the skills necessary for thoughtful discretion. It begins with a discussion of how the jury who convicted Socrates, a jury much maligned for its inability to appreciate philosophical truth, still exhibited the potential for radical enfranchisement. Then as now, the threat of a jury driven by prejudice undermines the integrity of the institution and of democracy writ large, but it continues to be a place where citizens have the opportunity to shape what punishment means and to complete the defining act of democracy, legislative self-authorization.

Socrates and the Jury

In the Athens of 399 BCE, democracy had been restored after a period of oligarchic rule, and the reforms of Solon, which included the right of all male citizens to vote in the assembly and serve on the jury, were central to the democratic functioning of the polis. In that context, Socrates, an elder of the community and long-standing teacher, was put on trial for impiety and corrupting the youth. Moreover, he was thought to be engaging in that secret tool for destroying democracy—sophistry—and was upending the moral conventions of society by making the weaker argument appear the stronger. Socrates denied the charges but was, indeed, no ardent supporter of democracy. He thought democratic culture had a tendency to produce lazy, hasty, and dim citizens, who were prone to following demagogues and enamored by public opinion. His skepticism extended to jurors who, as described by Plato in the *Gorgias*, he found idle and avaricious, motivated mainly by the stipend they received for service.[2] He may have been dependent on Athenian democracy to have the freedom to teach philosophy, but he was in deep conflict with its egalitarian tendencies. Socrates was brought to trial in front of the *dikasterion*, an assembly made up of five hundred citizens who swore "to vote according to the laws where there are laws, and where there [are] not, to vote as justly as in us lies."[3] During the trial Socrates defended himself by showing the contradictory and nonsensical nature of the claims made by his accuser; he refused to flatter the jury as that would have been contrary to his life's work of exposing the false idols of money and power within Athenian life. Both Xenophon's and Plato's accounts suggest that he was arrogant and boastful in his remarks, knowing that jurors would be agitated in hearing him talk about himself in superlative terms, backed by the sagacity of the Oracle at Delphi. One could say that he taunted the jurors to extend their considered judgment to his case despite making himself as unlikable as possible. He was, however, surprised by the outcome of voting, if not the verdict: the first vote (regarding conviction) was close, with 280 voting for the prosecution and 220 voting for the defense. This unexpectedly divided *dikasterion* powerfully captures the possibilities of critical thinking within a jury. The jurors in Socrates's case had every reason to blindly affirm the ideology of the ruling class: Socrates's accusers were of high status, and he foregrounded attacks on convention in a way that would have ramifications for all the propertied men who were serving. Furthermore, Socrates had also doubted the jurors' ability to do their job. A mob mentality stemming from a sense of their own self-preservation could easily have ruled the day and led to an overwhelming majority for the prosecution, but this did not happen. Just as the jury in the trial of Orestes at the founding of the Areopagus ended in an evenly split jury (with Athena called in to break the tie), the vote in Socrates's trial was close, suggesting that the institution of the jury may be one of the few places for authentic divergences of opinion in political life. In the contemporary era, the finality and singularity of the verdict necessarily obscures the debate that preceded it and suggests that public opinion is more extreme than it actually is. Yet, the closeness of the vote in Socrates's trial, under conditions ripe for prejudice, shows how influential a jury trial is as an opportunity for critical reflection on jurors' opinions and their perceived societal norms. Given the responsibility to decide the fate of another, jurors are poised to take the decisions asked of them more seriously than almost any others they make as citizens. They also have an opportunity to break with convention, and the pressure of public opinion that accompanies it, because a juror is expected to listen to multiple positions and come to a conclusion (although in the Athenian case this conclusion would have been reached individually without deliberation). Even if one knew how one was "supposed" to vote, there is always a moment of decision left to the juror alone. Radical enfranchisement imagines what can be done to prepare jurors to make the most of this moment of decision, including an understanding of the social dimensions of punishment.

The liberal tradition, while making punishment a central concern for the legitimacy of the state, has not necessarily connected it to its visions of citizenship. Take, for example, John Locke's defense of the execution of a thief, who must be judged not just for the theft but also for the moment of domination over the victim when other crimes were also possible. It is this threat of murder that justifies a wide range of punishment by the sovereign without resulting in an arbitrary application of the law (and is also present in contemporary self-defense arguments that hinge on biased perceptions).[4] Within such a Lockean model, the ever-present potential for excessive punishment sows a type of fear among the polity, not to mention a justification of such actions by the state, and allows the conceptual boundary between citizens and criminals to be maintained efficiently by citizens who never want to be subject to the violent excesses they know are possible. Citizens do this through cultural and social norms, including stigma and ostracization, but also through an avoidance of engagement with questions of punishment. "Can the state appear just even as it administers pain?" is a question that is often difficult to answer, but may be at the crux of the schism between citizenship and punishment that has characterized liberal democracy.[5] For Michel Foucault, the ideal of justice, its essence always a genealogical fallacy, is eviscerated when thinking about violence enacted by the state on the bodies of its citizens.[6] Punishment becomes a means of surveillance and a system of discipline with outcomes far removed from ideals of equality and liberty. The language of justice is a mask for the brutal actions of power-knowledge affecting all within its matrix and is unable to exist apart from it. That citizens choose not to embrace their role as deciders of punishment is both rational (because of its corrupt foundation) and futile because they are already implicated by the many vectors of power within collective life that authorize it, but creative resistance may take many forms. To refuse to be a juror is to refuse to be a legitimizing agent in a system that can never be anything other than a potent source of normalizing disciplinarity. Within a Foucauldian critique, jury service, from its very inception, has little to offer a vision of emancipation so untethered to the state. While Foucault's antistatist critique reveals the many good reasons why citizens, or humans rather, would choose to remain as distant as possible from the judgment that precedes punishment, his own activism in relation to the condition of prisons reveals how important the nexus of humanity and punishment is.[7]

Writing this chapter allowed me to experience the same anxiety about "supporting" the legitimacy of punishment that I imagine many a reluctant juror feels. The instinct to avoid being involved in punishment may be experienced as an alarm bell telling the listener to get as far away as possible from a decision which will leave no one satisfied. Penology is marked by a long history of social control through the construction of deviance and criminality, where various attempts to recognize the humanity of those accused of crimes are usually coupled with new forms of degradation. Further justifications for punishment within the context of democratic life are mired in hypocrisy because of the failure to enact the kinds of freedom democracy promises while at the same time making use of scapegoats to deflect attention from this fact. For those not already involved with criminal justice, getting involved with the decisions of punishment can only bring, in this context, reason for rebuke. Yet to remove oneself from any association with the criminal justice system is to engage in another version of curtailed citizenship. One of the tenets of democracy is the need to bolster the legitimacy gained from creating the norms under which we live, both directly (through referenda) and indirectly, through elected representatives and the president. Once those norms are in place, there is one more check by the people before the state is allowed to bring its force to bear on one of its own: the trial, including the decision of the jury. If one believes that a code of laws is necessary for the protection of rights and liberties, then one must acknowledge that there should be a process for determining what should be done when those laws are violated. Investigating and punishing such violations requires practical wisdom, and a key premise of radical enfranchisement has been that while it is an asset that jurors are not repeat-players in the criminal justice system, they should be better prepared for their service. Max Weber thought the jury was an irrational organization that would eventually be phased out to give way to the bureaucratic rationality of modern states, but its connection to a more personal form of justice is one of the most important reasons to strengthen it. The "irrational" aspects of the jury trial are what allow jurors to take both the particularity and the humanity of the defendant seriously. The work of punishment depends on practical wisdom, a skill that cannot be cultivated if jury service is not understood as a defining moment of citizenship and prepared for in that way.

The Juror Project workshop mentioned in the introduction is one possibility for letting jurors learn about their power and deepen their understanding of the decisions about punishment. Similar workshops at schools, libraries, and civic organizations could also include information about alternatives to imprisonment, such as mediation, community conferences, and mental health services. Expanding what is relevant to jury service is one way to make questions of adjudication and rehabilitation salient as responsibilities of citizenship, as they are closely tied to punishment. Radical enfranchisement does not fit neatly into either a liberal view of punishment, focusing on rights and deterrence, or a communitarian view, which considers punishment to offer the offender the chance to "recognize and repent the wrongs they have done, to reform themselves, and so to reconcile themselves with those they have wronged."[8] While such a communitarian perspective and the possibilities of restorative justice it embodies can emerge from jurors who have a sense of their power, the ethos of punishment within radical enfranchisement is about how a community shapes the intention, meaning, and application of the law. Attention to the moral characteristics of the defendant is important insofar as it may the basis for mercy or other types of discretion and may, when defendants are assessed collectively, be part of a move away from incarceration.

Calling on citizens to take responsibility for punishment may suggest that juries should be deciding punishment in all cases, not just in capital ones. Jenia Iontcheva and Albert Dzur make compelling cases for giving the responsibility of punishment to juries as a natural extension of the debate about the different ends of punishment that occurs during jury deliberation.[9] Giving jurors the ultimate decision about the duration of punishment would leave no room for doubt about the community's relationship to the act. Radical enfranchisement places the verdict, rather than the sentence, as the crux of these considerations because there is a value in having a clear moment of jury intervention that can be seen to be authorizing the use of force by the state—or not. It is notoriously difficult for individuals who have not experienced prison to decide between the implications of a five-year sentence versus a ten-year one, for example, and while judges are prone to their own biases, their range of experience with different defendants may be advantageous.[10] As civic education in preparation for jury service grows and includes education on alternatives to incarceration, a reform to allow jury sentencing (with the addition of these alternatives) would be a better reflection of the task of the jury.

Once one has accepted the social dimensions of punishment, the radical enfranchisement of jurors becomes possible. The skills discussed in these chapters do not happen all at once; they are activated by the framework of the trial (such as with the presumption of innocence) and still need the appropriate conditions if they are to be employed. The cases that follow demonstrate how jurors navigated their power and demonstrated the potential impact of a clearer understanding of the scope and purpose of their actions. To begin, the case of the Camden 28 exhibits many of the signs of a radically enfranchised jury: they understood that they were being called to adjudicate something beyond the charge itself, they (with the judge's guidance) saw the multifaceted role of the state at the trial, and they were able to incorporate varied aspects of civic life (urban renewal, FBI preventative strategies, the war in Vietnam) into their consideration of the verdict. These considerations may not always be appropriate, but this jury's ability to discern that it was appropriate to consider the larger political context is an example of the practical wisdom jurors must cultivate.

The Camden 28

While the other trials presented in this chapter paint the jury as lacking critical information for its decision about justice, the experience of the jury in the Camden 28 trial evinces many of the qualities of radical enfranchisement. The facts of the case are these: On August 22, 1971, a group of twenty-eight antiwar activists, including two Catholic priests and a Protestant minister, broke into the draft board office located on the fifth floor of the federal building in Camden, New Jersey.[11] There they attempted to destroy the paper records of all class 1-A draft registrants who had been cleared for unrestricted military service, but the attempt was foiled when they were caught by FBI agents who had been alerted to the plan by an informant active in the group. After rejecting the plea deal of a misdemeanor charge, seventeen participants were charged with seven felonies, including the destruction of government property and interfering with the Selective Service system. Each then faced more than forty years in prison. During the trial, some of the defendants chose to act as their own lawyers while others were classified as cocounsel alongside their attorneys, but all were deeply committed to crafting their defense as an extension of the political statement they had made with the destruction of the draft cards. The trial hinged on a defense of civil disobedience, that is, the defendants admitted that they had broken the law, but stipulated that they should not be punished because of their motivation to draw attention to the violence and degradation for which the US military was responsible in Vietnam. Furthermore, they could not be held entirely responsible for the nature of the action because the FBI had insured that the break-in would be carried out through the contributions of the informant, Bob Hardy. He had purchased the necessary equipment for the raid and taught the others techniques for furtive entry based on his experience as a general contractor. Father Michael Doyle captured the challenge to the jury in his opening statement for the defense:

> The terrible question that we try to put before you is simply this. Who went too far? Did the military go too far, by entering Vietnam and continuing in the war there for 12 years or more? Did the Camden 28 go too far in trying to stop it? Or did the FBI go too far in giving help to the defendants to make it possible in August of '71? And what does too far mean when the killing has started and you want to stop it?[12]

His formulation of "Who went too far?" captures the complexities of justice that a jury is expected to navigate. The FBI's techniques of entrapment were under scrutiny, particularly in light of the governmental secrecy that had recently been revealed through the Pentagon Papers and the burgeoning Watergate scandal, topics which Howard Zinn addressed in his testimony as a witness. Attending to the letter of the law would have been a parsimonious approach for the jury, but that was so clearly at odds with the complexity of the trial that the jurors were able to see that their role include a consideration of the appropriateness of punishment itself and the expansive conception of justice that entailed. The judge, Clarkson Fisher, encouraged the jurors to reflect on the broader context for punishment when he said the jury should consider the possibility of government overreach that "was offensive to the basic standards of decency and shocking to the universal sense of justice" when deciding the case. He explicitly denied the appropriateness of nullification, but, with his charge to the jury, one that radically enfranchised them as it were, Judge Fisher communicated his confidence in their ability to go beyond being "fact-finders" and pursue judgment about a just verdict in a way only laypeople could.

Bob Hardy, the informant, was a member of the Catholic Church and friendly with the circle of antiwar activists, and his motivations for alerting the FBI were not malicious. Not previously employed by the FBI, he wanted to protect his like-minded friends from putting themselves at risk for their cause and felt betrayed at what the FBI ultimately asked him to do. His affidavit, filed in 1972 prior to the trial, and his testimony during trial were remarkable in their blunt criticisms of the FBI. He wrote, "It is a case of manufacturing crimes to support repressive policies and the political futures of persons in power," and he detailed the extent to which the FBI both funded the Camden 28 operation and convinced him that the agency would intervene during the dry run of the action.[13] With Hardy's affidavit, another aspect of the radical enfranchisement of jurors comes into sharp relief, that of jurors as a check on the wide penumbra of the security state. Entrapment and sting operations are often justified as effective ways of combating terrorist activity, but the practice blurs the relationship between criminal activity and the incentives of law enforcement as keepers of the peace. When citizens are motivated to not only report on others but also provide opportunities to put criminal plans into action, they are rewarded for helping their peers to act in ways punishable by the state. The civic bonds of solidarity are broken. Laypeople who become involved in law enforcement and security as informers also have no recourse when the arrangement is violated by the FBI or other state institutions. In fact, they are more compromised than other citizens because officers of the state likely know of legal violations for which they could be held responsible. When criminal informants are recruited from prison, they are particularly vulnerable to accepting the assignment because of the implications for parole and employment opportunities after incarceration.[14] When asked to consider evidence based on the work of an informant, juries must again be reminded of the distinctive role they play as nonexperts and non-repeat-players in the courtroom. An orientation of radical enfranchisement provides a way to do this while not eschewing the task of judgment altogether. While the other officers of the court and in law enforcement have a vested interest in a guilty verdict to justify the effort and expense of a sting operation, the jury is the only body that can consider the extent of the state's role when making a decision about the meaning of justice in a particular case.

The Camden 28 case can be seen as a rare example of radical enfranchisement because of (1) the way in which the option of nullification was openly acknowledged by the judge (but presented as an undesirable option), alongside his call to scrutinize the state's actions, and (2) the way the jury was encouraged to think about what legitimate reasons for punishment might exist. The prosecution was able to challenge the scope of jury power directly and had the judge's backing in arguing that the case should not be a referendum on the war. The explicit nature of the exchange about the power of the jury contributes to a reading of it as consistent with radical enfranchisement. The case of the Camden 28 also speaks to how much of radical enfranchisement can be linked to larger movements of political literacy and a climate of civic action. The jurors in the case had been part of a national conversation about government secrecy and civil disobedience outside the courtroom, and in this way they had been educated about their power as citizens before the trial began. They were thus not entirely reliant on the arguments presented at trial for the context of the crime and had a heightened understanding of the dialogic interaction between lay and expert decision-making on questions of politics and law.

While it may appear that radical enfranchisement is a veil for advancing a liberal agenda in the courts, I return to the case of the Bundy family and the multiple trials that centered on Cliven Bundy's leadership in the occupation of federal lands. In a 2017 trial that ended with the judge declaring a mistrial because of Brady violations by the prosecution (for the withholding of evidence), jurors were asked during voir dire about their opinions on "guns, violence, the First and Second amendments, the media and federal authority," all timely political issues in the region and on conservative media outlets.[15] The jury pool also seemed to have many people who were concerned about a nearby proposed waste management facility pending Congressional approval and connected it to the case through the issue of federal control. The Bundy defense was strategic in how it positioned itself in relation to the authority of the federal government, at times denying it and at other times invoking it to protect the Second Amendment right to firearms.[16] As in previous trials with the Bundys as defendants, the defense team encouraged the jurors to send a larger message about state-federal relations through their verdict. The appeal to constitutionality by the defense suggests another reason for greater civic education. Still, the difficulty prosecutors had convicting the Bundys reveals a political reality that detractors from their mission should not easily dismiss. Attending to it will offer insights both for mobilizing social movements and for other types of legal violations that may occur, including those with victims other than federal agents. The Bundy jurors were radically enfranchised in their acute understanding of their power to influence the punishment of defendants they considered to be peers, but it is not clear that they went through the process of self-scrutiny necessary to fully inhabit the role.

The Central Park 5

One aspect of radical enfranchisement that is hard to decipher in the Camden 28 case but prominently lacking in the Central Park 5 is the turning of doubt inward as a way to mitigate the biases that jurors bring to the courtroom. The high status afforded to the clergy and their devoted followers in the Camden 28 likely helped the jurors see them as political actors fighting for a righteous cause, while the five teenagers falsely imprisoned in the Central Park case had an uphill battle to resist the strong media sentiment that they, or people who looked like them, must have committed the vicious crime in question.

There is perhaps no case that better captures how jurors reflect the political anxieties of race, class, and urban life than that of the Central Park jogger. In April of 1989, fifteen to twenty black and Latino teenagers entered Central Park through its 110th Street entrance, and a handful of them proceeded to harass, assault, and rob a homeless man and two joggers.[17] While some of the boys were being detained by police officers from the Central Park precinct, there were incoming reports of the savage beating and rape of twenty-eight-year-old Trisha Meili, an investment banker who lived on the Upper East Side and routinely jogged in the park. Immediately the teenagers became suspects, even though the time and location of those crimes were not reconcilable with what the police knew about their activity that night.[18] Kevin Richardson, Raymond Santana, Korey Wise, Yusuf Salaam, and Antron McCray, all juveniles between fourteen and sixteen years old and who did not know each other before their arrests, were each coerced by police officers into confessing participation, to various degrees, in the assault, robbery, attempted murder, and rape of the jogger. Over the course of two trials, all five were found guilty by juries and received sentences of five to fifteen years; four would serve seven years, and Wise would serve a longer sentence because he was tried as an adult. In 2002, an inmate serving a life sentence at Rikers Island for serial rape confessed to the crime, and DNA evidence, in the context of a new New York Police Department investigation, confirmed his involvement. Based on this new evidence, the Central Park 5 had their convictions vacated in 2002. In 2014, after a decade-long lawsuit based on their wrongful imprisonment, the City of New York settled the case for $40 million.[19] In hindsight, it is a powerful case that raises questions about the integrity of the prosecution and the ability of jurors to fully engage with the standard for reasonable doubt in light of the challenges of bias and the allure of (a faulty) narrative. At the time, it was a highly symbolic contest between a city that had been overtaken by "wilding" teenagers and law enforcement, with the jogger herself becoming what Joan Didion called a "sacrificial player in the sentimental narrative that is New York public life."[20]

While the highly publicized nature of the trial may have resulted in inferior investigative work in the rush to quell public fears, it also led to curiosity about the jurors' process. Ronald Gold, one of the jurors, told the *Manhattan Lawyer* that he was "deeply troubled by the discrepancies in the story McCray tells on his videotaped statement and the prosecution's scenario."[21] He goes on to say, "Why did McCray place the rape at the reservoir when all evidence indicated it happened at 102nd St.?" Another juror, Harold Brueland, writing in the *Daily News* after the trial, described how deeply contested the guilty verdict was in the jury room, especially on the attempted murder charge, where half the jurors were inclined to acquit five days into the deliberation. He explains, "One black juror felt some of us might have been motivated by vengeance—even though he acknowledged it was a terrible attack. He held out for acquittal on robbery and on the assault and rape counts against Yusuuf Salaam and Raymond Santana. I remember telling him that if this had happened to my own sister, I would not want the wrong person to be convicted."[22] Here, Brueland reveals that the jurors considered the danger of their attachment to a particular (erroneous) narrative based on vengeance and racial animosity, rather than the evidence, along with the distortions of truth by the prosecution that may have been enabled by racism. He also acknowledges the possibility of a third story of an unknown perpetrator and the danger of a wrongful conviction when such a story cannot be developed. The question that remains, then, is how did the state meet its burden of proof in the eyes of this jury?

The answer lies in the contradictions surrounding coercively obtained confessions from those suspected of a crime and the jury's response to them. As Peter Brooks has argued, the criminal justice system attempts to protect a defendant from coerced involuntary confession through the Miranda warning and the Fifth Amendment protection against self-incrimination, but at the same time allows law enforcement to be deceptive, misleading, and manipulative about evidence and punishment in the service of getting a statement of guilt from the suspect.[23] The contradiction is such that the Miranda warnings could even be thought to give police officers more protection for the unsavory methods used in the interrogation of defendants because the onus is on the suspect to know how to utilize the rights as they have been read to her. As Brooks explains, "A cynical interpretation of the Court's decision in Miranda would say that the Court cut the Gordian knot of the problem of voluntariness by saying to the police: if you follow these forms, we'll allow that the confession you obtained was voluntary."[24] One can interpret the events of the Central Park case as hewing to this exchange: the defendants were informed of their Miranda rights (they were even captured on video) but were still subject to lawyerless interrogation lasting between fourteen and thirty hours. This sequence of events gave the written confessions eventually extracted from each of them a veneer of legitimacy, despite their subsequent disavowals and the blatant incompatibility of the confessions with the material evidence.[25] It also reads as a textbook case of police interrogation popularized by John E. Reid: from the strategy of making it appear that the only way out of confinement was confession, to the statements in the suspects' handwriting with all names and events dictated by the officers, to the extreme dependency felt by the teenagers and their parents on the police officers for their eventual freedom, the police-dictated narrative became the only available option for the Central Park 5.[26] The validity of the confessions was almost immediately questioned because of the defendants' ages and the media frenzy surrounding the case, but the stain of a confession, even a false one, is difficult to erase.[27]

The lack of physical evidence, the discrepancies between the accounts given by the young men, and the nature of the crime (evidence from the scene indicated one perpetrator, not several) further suggested that the confessions were false. Yet, videotapes from the interrogation room, where the exhausted teenagers confessed to the crimes, were influential for the jury, and it is not hard to see why. Watching the video with the knowledge that the confessions were fabricated, it was still striking to me how convincingly they elaborated on details of the violent crime (e.g., Wise carefully described a rock used to attack the victim) and how they confirmed that they were not making the statements under duress, a pattern present in other cases of false confessions.[28] The details the defendants gave did not match many of the facts of the crime and they never talked about the location, for example, but the video shows how the defendants persuasively performed the false narrative they were provided. It also revealed that the interrogated teenagers had internalized that there was an incentive to be as detailed as possible in their false confessions because they believed that this would expedite their release.[29] While this case seems to be an obvious example of police-led fabrication, the challenge of separating authentic testimonies from mendacious ones stumps police officers and jurors alike. The myth that liars have telltale tics visible to the trained eye is pervasive, but the intuitions that lead experts and laypeople to determine whether or not someone is telling the truth are often wrong.[30] Thus, while following hunches and instincts about the veracity of testimony will always be a part of a juror's task, there is need for greater education about the conditions that give rise to false confessions and the scrutiny required by jurors whenever a confession is entered as evidence. This can be seen as a type of "corruption" of the juror's perception of an idealized form of police work and of the complexity of human behavior under duress. The civic education that is necessary for radical enfranchisement should include instruction about the prominence of false confessions and their impact because encounters with them during a case will always appear partisan and vulnerable to lawyerly distortion.

In addition to saying that their clients were the victims of a police witch hunt fueled by racism, the defense teams in both trials highlighted the implausible narrative of the prosecution's case and the fraudulent way in which the confessions were obtained.[31] After Kevin Richardson and Korey Wise were found guilty, Assistant District Attorney Robert Morgenthau responded to this strategy and said, "Once again the jury has rejected the spurious claims that the police manufactured evidence and used coercive tactics to obtain confessions."[32] It is hard to know how greater information about the existence of false confessions would have affected the jurors in the case, but an orientation of radical enfranchisement might have prepared jurors to more carefully consider the possibility. Not all claims of manufactured evidence are true, but the ability to assess such a claim relies on an understanding of the potential fallibility of police officers that is in tension with other conventions of court procedure. Radical enfranchisement provides a way to understand this fallibility alongside a respect for the integrity of the trial as an institution. It is an opportunity to uncover threads of narratives related to the crime or the defendant that have been lost along the way, especially in the extreme hierarchies of the interrogation room. The skepticism that jurors must entertain to make sense of a case that depends on confessions is best understood in the context of a productive tension between the jury and the officers of the court, a perspective that will likely be seen as partisan (and potentially dangerous in its affront to authority) when it appears during a trial. The Central Park 5 case highlights the role of the jury as a counterweight to the coercive power of the state that can be used to extract false confessions from defendants. Once a judge has allowed admissibility of a confession, it is only the jury that can call into question whether the spirit of the law was violated (as in the case of Miranda rights) and halt the momentum of the prosecution's case. The adversarial relationship between the jury and the judge discussed in chapter 1 must also extend to police officers. The Fifth Amendment privilege, while a critical part of the adversarial system, is not enough to offset the great power that police officers have and the difficulty defendants face in asserting these rights. The jury's role to protect against the tyranny of the state must also extend to protection against the tyranny of police officers, an issue at the center of the Movement for Black Lives.

One of the reforms implemented to curb false confessions in many states is the mandatory videotaping of interrogations, a procedural norm that is meant both to heighten police awareness of the best practices for questioning suspects and to provide a better factual record for judges and juries. Still, video evidence was not enough to alert the jury of the false confessions in the Central Park case; had the jury seen tape from the first two hours of questioning Korey Wise, rather than the last two, they may have inferred a different reality. Better documentation of the interrogation process is desirable but will not solve the problem. Additionally, Saul Kassin has argued for the increased presence of experts who explain to the jury research on the phenomenon.[33] While this would be in the spirit of radical enfranchisement, more awareness prior to the trial would be advantageous so that the jury considers the possibility of false confessions along with the other intellectual demands of reasonable doubt, even apart from its connection to the testimony of an expert witness during the trial.

The Case of Cecily McMillan

In some cases, the jury wants to split the difference between a guilty verdict and a plea for mercy in imprisonment. The case of the Occupy Wall Street activist, Cecily McMillan, is one such example. The jurors in that case may have benefited from greater foreknowledge of their tasks and powers, but they still found a way to make their concern about the sentence evident to the judge and, by extension, the public. They took responsibility for their verdict using one of the channels available to them. Education about nullification prior to the trial may not have changed the outcome (and perhaps for good reasons), but it would have given jurors a better sense about the extent of their power.

In March 2012, Cecily McMillan, a graduate student at the New School in New York City, was one of the protestors who returned to Zuccotti Park to mark the six-month anniversary of the beginning of the Occupy Wall Street protests and the impact that they had in bringing attention to the concerns of the "99%" and the pervasive impacts of income inequality.[34] The police demanded the protesters clear the area or risk being charged with trespassing. The sequence of events following this command were at the crux of her trial for assaulting a police officer, a felony second-degree offense. The prosecution claimed that she, unprovoked, elbowed a police officer after asking another officer, "Are you filming this?" McMillan said that she felt a policeman grab her by the breast and lift her off the ground, and that she responded by struggling to get away. It was only during this process that she elbowed the officer in the eye. Her medical condition after the altercation is also in dispute. In the transport van she had a ten-minute seizure, caught partially on videotape, but the prosecution suggested that she had faked the condition and the videotape was suppressed during trial. The jury, which deliberated for three hours and returned with a guilty verdict, had concerns about the appropriate sentence for the crime, which was to be issued by the judge. To this end, a group of nine jurors sent a letter to the judge, signed by Juror #2, reading: "We the jury petition the court for leniency in the sentencing of Cecily McMillan. We would ask the Court to consider the probation with community service. We feel that the felony mark on Cecily's record is punishment enough for this case and that it serves no purpose to Cecily or to society to incarcerate her for any amount of time. We also ask that you factor in your deliberation process that this request is coming from 9 of the 12 member jury."[35] On the reasoning behind this act, one juror said, "They felt bad. Most just wanted her to do probation, maybe some community service. But now what I'm hearing is seven years in jail? That's ludicrous. Even a year in jail is ridiculous."[36]

In the end, the judge sentenced her to ninety days in prison at Rikers Island and five years of probation, while waiving the $5000 fine. This type of communication between the jury and the judge lends credence to arguments made by Dzur and others that the only way for jurors to deliberate fully about their verdict is for them to have a more accurate sense of what sentencing will be and even to participate in it.[37] If we want jurors to take responsibility for the impact of their verdicts and consider what it means to legitimize punishment, greater knowledge about sentencing may be necessary. It is notable that one of the historical catalysts of nullification is the inevitability of a mandatory sentence (from the "three strikes" law, for example) that the jury feels is too harsh.[38] In that case, the jurors incorporate their knowledge of the sentence in determining their judgment about punishment, or, to put it another way, knowing the likely sentence makes real what the impact of their verdict will be and reminds them of their power to intervene. If they had been familiar with an orientation of radical enfranchisement, this jury's decision may or may not have been affected by greater awareness of their implicit biases (against protesters or police officers, for example) or by clarity about the power of nullification. Given that there were three jurors who did not sign the statement and who probably would not have been comfortable with a not guilty verdict, awareness of nullification may not have affected the verdict. Still, an orientation of radical enfranchisement might have prompted the jury to think about what it could do inside the courtroom, at the apex of its power, to influence the punishment for the defendant, and to state more explicitly to the court that the designation between guilty and not guilty they were offered did not fit their understanding of criminal behavior worthy of incarceration.

Whistleblowers and the Role of the Jury

Lastly, an education in radical enfranchisement prior to jury service might cause there to be more of an outcry when violations clearly in dialogue with changing social norms about legality and punishment are not brought to trial. The jury trial itself might take on a significance not currently granted, as with the case of whistleblowers. The role of juries as a check on the surveillance state is now a question inextricably tied to whistleblowers against the National Security Agency (NSA), Central Intelligence Agency (CIA), and other federal agencies. While the Obama administration increased legal protections for whistleblowers who experience retaliation after they reveal corruption, fraud, or other violations in the private sector, public sector employees are not afforded the same protection.[39] Eight individuals have been indicted since 2008 under the Espionage Act of 1917 for crimes connected to revealing information about the actions of the state to reporters, far more than in any previous administration.[40] Such a punitive response is noteworthy in part because of the ubiquity of official back-channel methods of communication, leaks in their own right, that all presidents have used as a way to communicate with the public. To prosecute leakers and whistleblowers because they went against conventional channels of communication highlights the variability of what it means to act in the public interest. The experience of John Kiriakou is emblematic of the strategy of prosecution

for whistleblowing pursued by the Obama administration, which has arguably led to a chilling effect on journalistic freedom.[41] After fourteen years
as a CIA officer, including a post in Pakistan as the chief counterterrorism
officer after the September 11 attacks, Kiriakou worked as a consultant for
ABC News. In a 2007 interview on that network, he was the first person to
publicly confirm that waterboarding was an interrogation method used by
the CIA and that he, personally, considered it to be a form of torture. In
2012, he was charged with releasing the name of a covert CIA operative to
a journalist (who did not publish it) and accepted a plea deal that resulted
in almost two years in prison plus a period of house arrest. The indictment
did not mention the ABC interview, but Kiriakou maintains that he was
targeted for his role in revealing the practice of torture by CIA officers. The
nature of the charge made it less likely that the jury would consider its role
in opposition to the dominance of the state, an orientation that affects the
defendant's assessment of the risk of a criminal trial. The success of the plea
deal also reveals the ways in which the possibility of the radical enfranchisement of jurors in whistleblower cases may be closed off.

In the most high-profile of the whistleblower cases, Edward Snowden
has been granted asylum in Russia as a way to avoid facing charges in the
United States for unauthorized communication of national defense information among other charges.[42] He and his lawyers have asked for the opportunity to present to a jury the defense that he acted in the public interest
and, were this to happen, it would be an extremely fruitful opportunity for a
discussion of the radical enfranchisement of jurors.[43] Imagining such a trial,
even if the term "nullification" is not mentioned by the judge or attorneys,
the value of laypeople (rather than security experts, for example) deciding
on the validity of the statute in this particular case and the nature of the
public interest would become evident. Even the federal government's apparent fear of a revived public conversation about Snowden's guilt suggests
how important a jury trial might be in redefining whistleblowing in relation
to civil disobedience.

Refusing the Honor of Punishment

In the early twentieth century, Emma Goldman offered a scathing critique of
the prison system in the United States, noting the vile conditions, exorbitant
expense, and its relationship to structural conditions of poverty for which
the state is to blame. While she does not address the role of jurors, she holds
all citizens to task for their understanding of criminality and misperceptions of incarceration as a necessary response when she writes, "With the

social consciousness wakened, the average individual may learn to refuse the 'honor' of being the bloodhound of the law. He may cease to persecute, despise, and mistrust the social offender, and give him a chance to live and breathe among his fellows."[44] The radical enfranchisement of jurors is this rethinking of the duty of those who have the power to punish, but it will take significant effort for us to become the citizens who are able and willing to do this work. The growing consensus about the consequences of mass incarceration make this an apt moment to transform the civic education of jurors and consider the possibilities gained when jurors know more about the challenges and demands of the trial process.

The fate of juries foreshadows the fate of democracy: if jurors can, with the guidance they receive through civic education and the trial, mitigate the obstacles of prejudice and bias to make more thoughtful decisions, it may be the best hope for their ability to make judgments as citizens.

NOTES

INTRODUCTION

1. Sidney Lumet, director; story by Reginald Rose, *12 Angry Men* (Los Angeles: Orion-Nova, 1957).

2. For good overviews of the jury process, see Jeffrey Abramson, *We, the Jury: The Jury System and the Ideal of Democracy* (Cambridge, MA: Harvard University Press, 2000); Akhil Amar, "Reinventing Juries: Ten Suggested Reforms," *UC Davis Law Review* 28 (1995): 1169–94; Robert P. Burns, *The Death of the American Trial* (Chicago: University of Chicago Press, 2009); Dennis D. Devine, *Jury Decision-Making: The State of the Science* (New York: NYU Press, 2012); R. A. Duff, *Trials and Punishment* (Cambridge: Cambridge University Press, 1986); Albert Dzur, Ian Loader, and Richard Sparks, eds., *Democratic Theory and Mass Incarceration* (New York: Oxford University Press, 2016); Andrew Guthrie Ferguson, *Why Jury Duty Matters* (New York: NYU Press, 2012); Dennis Hale, *The Jury in America: Triumph and Decline* (Lawrence: University Press of Kansas, 2016); Randolph N. Jonakait, *The American Jury System* (New Haven, CT: Yale University Press, 2003); Harry Kalven and Hans Zeisel, *The American Jury* (Chicago: University of Chicago Press, 1971); Nancy Marder, *The Jury Process* (New York: Foundation Press, 2005); Roger Roots, "The Rise and Fall of the American Jury," *Seton Hall Circuit Review* 8, no. 1 (2011): 1–42; Melissa Schwartzberg, *Counting the Many: The Origins and Limits of Supermajority Rule* (New York: Cambridge University Press, 2014).

3. For a trenchant look at the divergences between US and European sentencing practices, see Joshua Kleinfeld, "Two Cultures of Punishment," *Stanford Law Review* 68, no. 5 (2016): 933–1037.

4. See Jenia Iontcheva, "Jury Sentencing as Democratic Practice," *Virginia Law Review* 89, no. 2 (2003); Albert W. and Rekha Mirchandani Dzur, "Punishment and Democracy: The Role of Public Deliberation," *Punishment and Society* 9, no. 2 (2007): 151–75; Albert Dzur, *Punishment, Participatory Democracy, and the Jury* (Oxford: Oxford University Press, 2012).

5. R. M. Dworkin, "Is Law a System of Rules?," in *The Philosophy of Law*, ed. R. M. Dworkin (Oxford: Oxford University Press, 1977), 52.

6. The project primarily focuses on criminal trials rather than civil trials because of their singular role in the task of punishment. The state's monopoly over the legitimate use of violence extends to the legitimate use of punishment as a response to an infraction

of the legal code under the auspices of constitutional protections within a liberal democracy.

7. Tony Honoré, *Ulpian* (Oxford: Oxford University Press, 1982).

8. While standard jury instructions ask jurors to set aside compassion when considering the verdict, Linda Ross Meyer presents a view that asserts its legitimacy as a basis, alongside others, for mercy by executives, legislators, judges, and jurors. In contrast to a defense of retributive justice and rule of law, Meyer extrapolates on the "connectedness, embeddedness and finitude that undergird community and government, and that come before reason and serve as the basis and touchstone for judgments about justice that are abstracted in law." The connectedness of community that makes up the basis for judgment about punishment in her account is consistent with the perspective presented here. Linda Ross Meyer, "The Merciful State," in *Forgiveness, Mercy, and Clemency*, ed. Austin Sarat and Nasser Hussain (Stanford, CA: Stanford University Press, 2007), 65.

9. See, e.g., Michelle Alexander, *The New Jim Crow* (New York: New Press, 2010); Marie Gottschalk, *Caught: The Prison State and the Lockdown of American Politics* (Princeton, NJ: Princeton University Press, 2016); Angela Y. Davis, *Are Prisons Obsolete?* (New York: Seven Stories Press, 2005); Bernard Harcourt, "Abolition in the U.S.A. by 2050: On Political Capital and Ordinary Acts of Resistance," in *Road to Abolition?*, ed. Austin Sarat and Charles Ogletree (New York: NYU Press, 2009).

10. For more on liberalism and punishment, see Keally McBride, *Law, Meaning, and Violence: Punishment and Political Order* (Ann Arbor: University of Michigan Press, 2009). In addition, Andrew Dilts has shown that felony disenfranchisement defines boundaries of political membership and shores up systemic practices of racism by tying punishment to a negated form of citizenship. Andrew Dilts, *Punishment and Inclusion: Race, Membership, and the Limits of American Liberalism* (New York: Fordham University Press, 2014).

11. For more information, see www.thejurorproject.org.

12. Scott E. Sundby, *A Life and Death Decision: A Jury Weighs the Death Penalty* (New York: St. Martin Griffin, 2005).

13. Anthony Giacchino, *The Camden 28*, DVD, directed by Anthony Giacchino, New York: First Run Features (2007); Matt Zoller Seitz, "A Draft-Board Break-in That Put Activism on Trial," *New York Times*, July 27, 2007; Donald Janson, "Camden 28 Jury Asks Re-Reading," *New York Times*, May 19, 1973; Mark Edward Lender, *This Honorable Court: The United States District Court for the District of New Jersey, 1789–2000* (New Brunswick, NJ: Rutgers University Press, 2006).

14. For more on how a community's conflict with the criminal code can erode compliance with the law, see Paul H. Robinson and John M. Darley, *Justice, Liability, and Blame: Community Views and the Criminal Law* (Boulder, CO: Westview Press, 1995).

15. Empirical evidence from states that allow jurors to be involved in sentencing in noncapital cases suggests that jurors are not always more lenient than judges, exhibiting more variation in responses to similar crimes and longer sentences for all major categories of felonies. Simply giving jurors power over sentencing will not lead to lesser punishments and this is not the argument here. Nancy King and Roosevelt Noble, "Jury Sentencing in Non-Capital Cases: Comparing Severity and Variance with Judicial Sentences in Two States," *Journal of Empirical Legal Studies* 2, no. 2 (2005): 331–67.

16. King and Noble.

17. For a reading of the power of the jury embedded in the Magna Carta, see Lysander Spooner, *An Essay on the Trial by Jury* (Boston: John P. Jewett, 1852). For a good description of the evolution of the modern jury, see Hale, *Jury in America*.

18. Marianne Constable, *The Law of the Other: The Mixed Jury and Changing Conception of Citizenship, Law, and Knowledge* (Chicago: University of Chicago Press, 1993).

19. See, e.g., *Duncan v. Louisiana*, 391 US 145 (1968), which required jury trials at the state level based on the due process clause of the Fourteenth Amendment, and *Taylor v. Louisiana*, 419 US 522 (1975), which held that a jury drawn from a fair cross-section of the community could not exclude women from the venire. *Batson v. Kentucky*, 476 US 79 (1986) continues to be the most important precedent for challenging race-based juror dismissals, even when new evidence on such dismissals emerges after the trial has ended.

20. Pauline Gregg, *Free-Born John: A Biography of John Lilburne* (London: Harrap, 1961).

21. Jason Frank shows how the very idea of the "people" underwent a transformation in the prerevolutionary era that set the stage for future action in their name. He writes, "The people went from a reserved, deferential, and passive body whose interests could be represented without their direct say to a demanding and 'taking' people forever jealous of their governors' power. In these prerevolutionary debates over political representation, the people became simultaneously more ambiguous and more powerful; the power attributed to the people expanded alongside their increasing unlocatability." Jason Frank, *Constituent Moments: Enacting the People in Postrevolutionary America* (Durham, NC: Duke University Press, 2009), 15.

22. Even for jury advocates who question its role in deciding on the law, the jury is often celebrated for its "common sense," as a shorthand reference to the benefits laypeople are expected to bring to their service. Yet, as Sophia Rosenfeld shows in her political history of the term, to evoke "common sense" is to suggest that what is contained within is already shared by a majority of people, even when this is not the case. Moreover, she argues that common sense "always belongs to the language of reaction, which is to say opposition" and is most often invoked during times of rapid change as a way to assert traditional values that can be the conduit for the entrenchment of prejudices. Taking these insights about common sense and applying them to the jury, it becomes clear that asking the jury to use their "common sense" is, in many ways, an empty command that could encourage a type of oppositional response to the presumption of innocence on which the adversarial trial relies and minimize the possibility that there could be legitimate disagreement on the outcome. Sophia Rosenfeld, *Common Sense: A Political History* (Cambridge, MA: Harvard University Press, 2011).

23. "Both before and during the revolution, colonial jury practices and the vision of law that underpinned them went much further than their English counterparts of a century earlier. Implicit in colonial pamphlets and jural claims, a profoundly innovative, even instrumental, understanding of law can be seen at work." Shannon Stimson, *The American Revolution in the Law: Anglo-American Jurisprudence before John Marshall* (Princeton, NJ: Princeton University Press, 1990), 5.

24. Kramer vividly recounts what popular constitutionalism looked like in the colonial era in a way that challenges current assumptions about law and politics. Larry D. Kramer, *The People Themselves: Popular Constitutionalism and Judicial Review* (New York: Oxford University Press, 2004).

25. While they suggest that the role of professionalization is overblown in the increase in plea bargains, McConville and Mirsky describe the dynamic as follows: "The new

police were capable of producing reliable evidence of guilt and, with the emergence of lawyers who had the ability to assess evidence, courtroom actors were able to distinguish between cases where conviction was certain and those where triable issues remained. In a context of cost-efficiency, everyday cases without triable issues gave rise to and became fodder for the guilty plea system." They also explore more contextual arguments suggesting that plea bargains were a type of ameliorative gesture that the elite used to placate the underclass. Mike McConville and Chester L. Mirsky, *Jury Trials and Plea Bargaining: A True History* (London: Hart Publishing, 2005), 2.

26. Erica Goode, "Stronger Hand for Judges in the Bazaar of Plea Deals," *New York Times*, March 22, 2012; also cited in Missouri v. Frye (2012).

27. Benjamin Weiser, "Trial by Jury, a Hallowed American Right, Is Vanishing," *New York Times*, August 7, 2016.

28. Albert W. Alschuler, "Plea Bargaining and Its History," *Columbia Law Review* 79, no. 1 (1979).

29. For a thorough consideration of the political, legal, and economic causes and consequences of the decline, see Burns, *Death of the American Trial*.

30. Sheldon Wolin, "Fugitive Democracy," *Constellations* 1, no. 1 (1994).

31. Wolin.

32. Frank, *Constituent Moments*, 8.

33. Jan-Werner Muller, *What Is Populism?* (Philadelphia: University of Pennsylvania Press, 2016).

34. John Pratt, *Penal Populism* (London: Routledge, 2008). See also Margaret Canovan, *Populism* (New York: Houghton Mifflin Harcourt, 1981).

35. For more on how thoroughly crime has become the organizing focus for political life, including through funding, policy, and the attitudes of elected officials, see Jonathan Simon, *Governing through Crime* (New York: Oxford University Press, 2007).

36. King and Noble, *Jury Sentencing*.

37. Franklin E. Zimring, Gordon Hawkins, and Sam Kamin, *Punishment and Democracy: Three Strikes and You're Out in California* (New York: Oxford University Press, 2001).

38. Albert Dzur, "The Myth of Penal Populism," *Journal of Speculative Philosophy* 24, no. 4 (2010): 370.

39. Burns's description of the received view is a nuanced consideration of another framework for understanding the trial. Robert Burns, *A Theory of the Trial* (Princeton, NJ: Princeton University Press, 1999).

40. For a pointed consideration of trials and democratic failure, see Lida Maxwell, *Public Trials: Burke, Zola, and Arendt on the Politics of Lost Causes* (New York: Oxford University Press, 2015).

41. Jacques Rancière, *Dissensus: On Politics and Aesthetics* (London: Continuum International Publishing Group, 2010), 38.

42. Rancière, 38.

43. Rancière, 31.

44. For more on this, see Peter Stone, *Lotteries in Public Life* (Charlottesville, VA: Imprint Academic, 2011); Norman J. Finkel, *Commonsense Justice: Jurors' Notions of the Law* (Cambridge, MA: Harvard University Press, 2009).

45. For more on the ways democratic theory has been underutilized for thinking about mass incarceration and its alternatives, see Dzur, Loader, and Sparks, *Democratic Theory and Mass Incarceration*.

46. See, e.g., Philip Pettit, "Is Criminal Justice Politically Feasible?," *Buffalo Criminal Law Review* 5, no. 2 (2002). For an argument about the proliferation of other forms of

adjudication and their potential desirability over juries, see Judith Reznik, "Migrating, Morphing, and Vanishing: The Empirical and Normative Puzzles of Declining Trial Rates in Court," *Journal of Empirical Legal Studies* 1, no. 3 (November 2004).

47. James Surowiecki, *The Wisdom of Crowds* (New York: Anchor, 2005). Hélène Landemore, "Democratic Reason: The Mechanism of Collective Intelligence in Politics," in *Collective Wisdom: Principles and Mechanisms*, ed. Hélène Landemore and Jon Elster (Cambridge: Cambridge University Press, 2012); and Hélène Landemore, *Democratic Reason: Politics, Collective Intelligence, and the Rule of the Many* (Princeton, NJ: Princeton University Press, 2013).

48. Kalven and Zeisel, *American Jury*.

49. G. K. Chesterton, "The Twelve Men," in *Tremendous Trifles* (New York: Dodd, Mead, 1920), 85; emphasis added.

50. It is interesting to note that in Shklar's influential categorization of the Aristotelian (rule by reason) and Montesquieuian (a check on elite power and arbitrary violence) interpretations of the rule of law, she highlights that "the rationality of judging, divorced from the ethical and political setting in which [Aristotle] described it, becomes as improbable as the liberal archetype when it is ripped out of its context." An orientation of radical enfranchisement can thus be seen as part of the ethical and political context for judgment, one that is in fact necessary for an understanding of the rule of law. Judith Shklar, "Political Theory and Rule of Law," in *Political Thought and Political Thinkers* (Chicago: University of Chicago Press, 1998), 32.

51. Whereas politics for Schmitt is defined by the friend/enemy distinction as the state articulates it, and Schmitt is careful to distinguish between the enemy and the criminal, the jury has the responsibility of demarcating the binary in a criminal trial. Tim Delaune, "Democratizing the Criminal: Jury Nullification as Exercise of Sovereign Discretion over the Friend-Enemy Distinction" (PhD diss., University of Massachusetts, Amherst, 2013); Carl Schmitt, *The Concept of the Political* (Chicago: University of Chicago Press, 1996).

52. The argument for the sovereignty of the jury cannot be reduced to Schmittian decisionism, however, because of the emphasis on procedure and the integrity of the adversarial process.

53. Alasdair MacIntyre, *After Virtue* (South Bend, IN: University of Notre Dame Press, 1981).

54. For more on the demands of civic education and its role in democracy, see Amy Guttman, *Democratic Education* (Princeton, NJ: Princeton University Press, 1999).

55. Mark W. Bennett, "Unraveling the Gordian Knot of Implicit Bias in Jury Selection: The Problems of Judge-Dominated Voir Dire, the Failed Promise of *Batson*, and Proposed Solutions," *Harvard Law and Policy Review* 4 (2010): 1207–29; John Gastil et al., *The Jury and Democracy: How Jury Deliberation Promotes Civic Engagement and Political Participation* (New York: Oxford University Press, 2010); Sheri Johnson, "Black Innocence and the White Jury," *Michigan Law Review* 83, no. 7 (1985): 1611–1707.

56. In *Batson v. Kentucky* 476 US 79 (1986) the Supreme Court found that removing jurors solely on the basis of race was in violation of the Sixth and Fourteenth Amendments.

57. *Foster v. Chatman* 578 US 14-8349 (2016).

58. James Forman Jr., *Locking up Our Own: Crime and Punishment in Black America* (New York: Farrar, Straus, and Giroux, 2017).

59. Forman, 237.

60. Mortimer R. Kadish and Sanford H. Kadish, *Discretion to Disobey: A Study of Lawful Departures from Legal Rules* (Stanford, CA: Stanford University Press, 1973); Mortimer R. Kadish and Sanford H. Kadish, "The Institutionalization of Conflict: Jury Acquittals," in *Law, Justice and the Individual in Society: Psychological and Legal Issues*, ed. June Louin Tapp and Felice J. Levine (New York: Holt, Rinehart, and Winston, 1977).

61. See also Paul Butler, "Racially Based Jury Nullification: Black Power in the Criminal Justice System," *Yale Law Journal* 105 (1995): 677–725.

62. Howe's still influential 1939 historical review of state-level jurisprudence shows how cyclical and repetitive the arguments for and against nullification are and the conflict the topic engenders among legal scholars and judges. Mark Dewolfe Howe, "Juries as Judges of Criminal Law," *Harvard Law Review* 52, no. 582, 613–48 (1939). For a perspective skeptical of the historical precedent, see Stanton D. Krauss, "An Inquiry into the Right of Criminal Juries to Determine the Law in Colonial America," *Journal of Criminal Law and Criminology* 89 (1998): 111–213.

63. According to a widely cited article by Darryl Brown, nullification is justified if it (1) discourages a separate, illegal act by government officials, (2) responds to a law that was enacted by a racist government structure, or (3) fulfills the Supreme Court's hope for the future legitimacy of the law as nullification signals unjust enforcement that should be remedied. While he pointedly responds to the most vociferous criticism of jury nullification (that it is outside of the rule of law and a precursor to chaos), it seems to be too narrow an approach to assessing the legitimacy of jury decisions. Brown's justification for nullification endows jurors with the skills of apprentice legal scholars, able to identify infractions of the rule of law at stages prior to the trial and then able to use the power of nullification as a corrective measure. Such an expectation asks the jury to do the work of long-term thinking about justice, a type of thinking for which the trial process is not particularly well-suited. Darryl K. Brown, "Jury Nullification within the Rule of Law," *Minnesota Law Review* 81, no. 5 (May 1997): 1149–1200.

64. Andrew Murphy, "Trial Transcript as Political Theory: Principles and Performance in the Penn-Mead Case," *Political Theory* 41, no. 6 (2013): 775–808.

CHAPTER ONE

1. US Const. amend. VI.

2. Dennis D. Devine, *Jury Decision-Making: The State of the Science* (New York: NYU Press, 2012); Gary J. Jacobsohn, "The Unanimous Verdict: Politics and the Jury Trial," *Washington University Law Quarterly* 1 (1977): 39–60; Edward P. Schwartz and Warren F. Schwartz, "Decisionmaking by Juries under Unanimity and Supermajority Voting Rules," *Georgetown Law Journal* 80 (1991–92): 775–808.

3. Alexis de Tocqueville, *Democracy in America*, ed. Harvey C. Mansfield and Debra Winthrop (Chicago: University of Chicago Press, 2000), bk. 1.16.

4. Tocqueville, bk. 1.2.8.

5. Tocqueville.

6. For more on the judge's power to direct the jury, see Hugo Black's dissent in *Galloway v. US*, 319 US 372 (1943).

7. Alexis de Tocqueville, *The Old Regime and the Revolution*, ed. François Furet and Françoise Melonio (Chicago: University of Chicago Press, 1998), 230.

8. Tocqueville, *Old Regime*, 232; emphasis added.

9. Tocqueville, *Democracy in America*, 1.1.6.

10. Jeffrey Abramson, *We, the Jury: The Jury System and the Ideal of Democracy* (Cambridge,

MA: Harvard University Press, 2000), 73; Randolph N. Jonakait, *The American Jury System* (New Haven, CT: Yale University Press, 2003), 23.

11. James Q. Whitman, "What Happened to Tocqueville's America?," *Social Research* 74, no. 2 (2007): 251–68.

12. Robert Burns argues that this is the alchemy of the trial and the format permits an unusual opportunity for a nuanced consideration of values. Robert Burns, *A Theory of the Trial* (Princeton, NJ: Princeton University Press, 1999).

13. Sheldon Wolin, *Tocqueville between Two Worlds: The Making of a Political and Theoretical Life* (Princeton, NJ: Princeton University Press), 534.

14. Albert Dzur, "Democracy's 'Free School': Tocqueville and Lieber on the Value of the Jury," *Political Theory* 38, no. 5 (2010): 603–30; Albert Dzur, *Punishment, Participatory Democracy, and the Jury* (Oxford: Oxford University Press, 2012).

15. Dzur, "Democracy's 'Free School,'" 605.

16. Thomas Hobbes, *Leviathan* (Indianapolis, IN: Hackett, 1994), Ch. 26.

17. Richard Tuck, "Hobbes and the Jury," unpublished work (2011).

18. Dzur, "Democracy's 'Free School.'"

19. Andrew Murphy, "Trial Transcript as Political Theory: Principles and Performance in the Penn-Mead Case," *Political Theory* 41, no. 6 (2013): 775–808.

20. Shannon Stimson, *The American Revolution in the Law: Anglo-American Jurisprudence before John Marshall* (Princeton, NJ: Princeton University Press, 1990), 62.

21. Tocqueville, *Democracy in America*, 1.2.8.

22. Robert Cover, "Violence and the Word," *Yale Law Journal* 95 (1986): 1601–31.

23. Cover, 1613; emphasis added.

24. Tocqueville, *Democracy in America*, 2.3.9.

25. Tocqueville, *Democracy in America*, 2.3.10.

26. Tocqueville, *Democracy in America*, 2.3.10.

27. See, e.g., Laura Janara, "Democracy's Family Values," in *Feminist Interpretations of Alexis De Tocqueville*, ed. Jill Locke and Eileen Hunt Botting (University Park, PA: Penn State University Press, 2008).

28. Tocqueville, *Democracy in America*, 2.3.12.

29. Delba Winthrop, "Tocqueville's American Woman and 'the True Conception of Democratic Progress,'" *Political Theory* 14, no. 2 (1986): 245.

30. Laura Janara, "Democracy's Family Values," in *Feminist Interpretations of Alexis De Tocqueville*, ed. Jill Locke and Eileen Hunt Botting (University Park, PA: Penn State University Press, 2008), 64.

31. Tocqueville, *Democracy in America*, 1.15.

CHAPTER TWO

1. In contrast to the secrecy surrounding the power of the jury to nullify, the recitation of the Allen Charge is meant to give jurors an even more potent sense of their power. When a judge says, "no other twelve people can do a better job than you," jurors realize how critical each of their voices is and the authority of their decision. The fears of anarchy, so present in fears surrounding jury nullification, are not present in concerns regarding the Allen Charge or the concerns raised by a hung jury. Nancy Marder, "The Myth of the Nullifying Jury," *Northwestern University Law Review* 93 (1999): 877–959; Alan W. Scheflin, "Jury Nullification: The Right to Say No," *Southern California Law Review* 45 (1972): 168–226; Christopher C. Schwan, "Right up to the Line: The Ethics of Advancing Nullification Arguments to the Jury," *Journal of the Legal Profession* 29 (2004–5): 293–304.

2. *Thaggard v. United States*, 354 F.2d 735 (1965).

3. Mark Lanier and Cloud Miller III, "The Allen Charge: Expedient Justice or Coercion?," *American Journal of Criminal Justice* 25, no. 1 (2000): 31–40.

4. For the American Bar Association's concerns surrounding the Allen Charge, see American Bar Association, "The Allen Charge Dilemma," *American Criminal Law Review* 10 (1972).

5. I also share with Burns the tone of my analysis: it is explicitly interpretive and normative, and not meant as an account of the law as understood by its practitioners or in the case law. Robert Burns, *A Theory of the Trial* (Princeton, NJ: Princeton University Press, 1999).

6. Gary J. Jacobsohn, "The Right to Disagree: Judges, Juries, and the Administration of Criminal Justice in Maryland," *Washington University Law Review* 4 (1976): 572.

7. I agree with Martha Merrill Umphrey's critique that Burns underestimates the fragility of such an idealized interpretation of the trial but, as I will argue below, an appreciation of the legitimacy of the hung jury decision and of the conditions that threaten it highlight the fragility of jury decisions, while preserving a complex understanding of their judging power. Martha Merrill Umphrey, "Fragile Performances: The Dialogics of Judgment in a Theory of the Trial," *Law and Social Inquiry* 28, no. 2 (2003): 527–32.

8. The impossibility of consensus on a variety of central issues of concern, especially those defining the "good life," leads critics like Moon to prefer bracketing them as well as paying attention only to those who are affected by a particular issue. Habermas himself makes the distinction between moral and political questions more defined in his later work. J. Donald Moon, "Practical Discourse and Communicative Ethics," in *Cambidge Companion to Habermas*, ed. Stephen K. White (Cambridge: Cambridge University Press, 2006).

9. Jürgen Habermas, *Moral Consciousness and Communicative Action* (Cambridge, MA: MIT Press, 2001); Jürgen Habermas, *Between Facts and Norms: Contributions to a Discourse Theory of Law and Democracy* (Cambridge, MA: MIT Press, 1998).

10. James Bohman, "Critical Theory and Democracy," in *Handbook of Critical Theory*, ed. David M. Rasmussen (Oxford: Blackwell, 1996), 203.

11. Habermas, *Moral Consciousness and Communicative Action*, 66.

12. For a discussion on jurors' ability to understand highly technical subject matter, see Neil Vidmar and Valerie P. Hans, *American Juries: The Verdict* (Amherst, NY: Prometheus Books, 2007), 153.

13. Wellmer has critiqued Habermas for suggesting that the formal requirements of the Ideal Speech Situation are erroneously posited as resulting in truth (and captured by the consensus theory of truth). I am sympathetic to these concerns, which are picked up in a different guise by proponents of a revised majority decision rule for juries, but the concerns do not derail the more important legitimizing function of Habermas's framework. Fundamentally, it is not some abstract truth that is sought through jury deliberation, but an adjudication of the evidence relevant to the charge at hand as the basis for the state's suspension of the rights of the defendant. How a jury of one's peers contingently determines justice in a particular situation is more important than confidence in the consensus theory of truth. Albrecht Wellmer, "Ethics and Dialogue," in *The Persistence of Modernity: Essays on Aesthetics, Ethics and Postmodernism* (Cambridge: Polity Press, 1991).

14. Cf. *Apodaca v. Oregon*, 406 US 404 (1972). *Johnson v. Louisiana*, 400 US 356 (1972). Unanimous juries do, however, need at least six jurors; *Ballew v. Georgia*, 435 US 223 (1978).

15. Gary J. Jacobsohn, "The Unanimous Verdict: Politics and the Jury Trial," *Washington University Law Quarterly* 1 (1977): 39–57; Michael Saks, "The Smaller the Jury, the Greater the Unpredictability," *Judicature* 79 (1996): 263–65.

16. Peter J. Coughlan, "In Defense of Unanimous Jury Verdicts: Mistrials, Communication, and Strategic Voting," *American Political Science Review* 94, no. 2 (2000): 375–93.

17. "Juries required to reach unanimity deliberating longer and in more ideal fashion than juries that were not required to reach complete agreement. Specifically, unanimous juries discussed key facts to a greater extent, touched on more case facts than two-thirds quorum juries, corrected mistaken assertions by members more often, elicited the participation of minority-view jurors to a greater extent, and ultimately produced a higher level of member satisfaction." Dennis D. Devine, *Jury Decision-Making: The State of the Science* (New York: NYU Press, 2012), 45.

18. It is reported that 10 percent of trials result in a verdict that is the opposite of a jury's original preferences, suggesting the substantial influence of the process of deliberation on assessments jurors had made individually during the trial. For discussion of the implications of a verdict-driven jury style versus an evidence-driven one, see John Gastil et al., *The Jury and Democracy: How Jury Deliberation Promotes Civic Engagement and Political Participation* (New York: Oxford University Press, 2010), 95.

19. I acknowledge that a Habermasian dissent based on (U) would assert that the proposal in question does not advance the interests of all and the interest of the speaker and this standard is at odds with what juries are asked to do.

20. D. Graham Burnett, *A Trial by Jury* (New York: Alfred A. Knopf, 2001).

21. Chambers suggests that the demand for closure in the form of a vote, formal decision, etc. always dramatically reduces the opportunity for nonstrategic deliberation. She does not see any way to bridge the gap but rather suggests that a balance be struck between deliberation and closure. Simone Chambers, "Discourse and Democratic Practices," in *Cambridge Companion to Habermas*, ed. Stephen K. White (Cambridge: Cambridge University Press, 2006).

22. Iris Marion Young, "Impartiality and the Civic Public: Some Implications of Feminist Critiques of Moral and Political Theory," *Praxis International* 5, no. 4 (1986): 394.

23. William Rehg, "Habermas's Discourse Theory of Law and Democracy: An Overview of the Argument," in *Handbook of Critical Theory*, ed. David M. Rasmussen (Oxford: Blackwell, 1996); Stephen K. White, *Recent Work of Jürgen Habermas: Reason, Justice, and Modernity* (Cambridge: Cambridge University Press, 1988); James Bohman, "'System' and 'Lifeworld': Habermas and the Problem of Holism," *Philosophy and Social Criticism* 15 (1989): 381–401.

24. Habermas, *Moral Consciousness and Communicative Action*, 138.

25. The situation of disagreement when there are shared lifeworlds is a liminal case for the interpretation I am suggesting. It may not be a mistake in the sense of failed good-faith deliberation, nor a politically significant impasse (because of lifeworld conflict), but rather a situation where reasonable jurors disagree on how to weight the evidence or to index the different norms.

26. Nicholas Rescher, *Pluralism: Against the Demand for Consensus* (Oxford: Oxford University Press, 1995); Lynn Sanders, "Against Deliberation," *Political Theory* 25, no. 3 (1997): 347–76; Seyla Benhabib, *Situating the Self* (Cambridge: Polity Press, 1992).

27. Jürgen Habermas, "Civil Disobedience: Litmus Test for the Democratic Constitutional State," *Berkeley Journal of Sociology* 30 (1985): 95–116.

28. Habermas, "Civil Disobedience."

29. Stephen K. White and Evan Robert Farr, "'No-Saying' in Habermas," *Political Theory* 40, no. 1 (2012).

30. White and Farr, 51.

31. Lasse Thomassen, "Communicative Reason, Deconstruction and Foundationalism: A Response to White and Farr," Political Theory 41, no. 3 (2013): 482–88.

32. Thomassen, 486.

33. In her writing about jury sentencing, Iontcheva sees great value in the Habermasian deliberative model for thinking about the purposes of punishment. While decisions about guilt, she argues, are more technocratic in how they expect jurors to line up evidence with legal calculations about doubt, the purpose of punishment and its manifestation in sentencing requires much more of a juror's individual worldview, or in my application of Habermasian language, the inherited and imbibed perspectives of a particular lifeworld that speak to rehabilitation and retribution. Jenia Iontcheva, "Jury Sentencing as Democratic Practice," *Virginia Law Review* 89, no. 2 (2003): 311–81.

34. Jeffrey Abramson, *We, the Jury: The Jury System and the Ideal of Democracy* (Cambridge, MA: Harvard University Press, 2000), xi.

35. Judith Butler, "Endangered/Endangering: Schematic Racism and White Paranoia," in *Reading Rodney King/Reading Urban Uprising*, ed. Robert Gooding-Williams (New York: Routledge, 1993).

36. Butler, 19.

37. Young, "Impartiality and the Civic Public."

38. Burns might be skeptical about the direct relationship I am asserting between lifeworld and juror decisions in the case of a hung jury. His interpretation suggests that there are many other areas of consideration before a juror makes a decision, not to mention the fact that experiencing the trial in all of its complexity challenges the lifeworlds of jurors in a multiplicity of ways. However, Burns highlights that part of a juror's role is to decide between competing norms and ways of judging; it is plausible to see how jurors might disagree on this because of lifeworld expectations. Burns, *A Theory of the Trial.*

39. Nancy Fraser, "Rethinking the Public Sphere: A Contribution to the Critique of Actually Existing Democracy," in *Habermas and the Public Sphere*, ed. Craig Calhoun (Cambridge, MA: MIT Press, 1992).

40. Vicki L. Smith and Saul M. Kassin, "Effects of the Dynamite Charge on the Deliberations of Deadlocked Mock Juries," *Law and Human Behavior* 17, no. 6 (1993): 625–43.

41. Martin F. Kaplan and Charles E. Miller, "Group Decision Making and Normative Versus Informational Influence: Effects of Type of Issue and Assigned Decision Rule," *Journal of Personality and Social Psychology* 53, no. 2 (1987): 306–13.

42. Smith and Kassin, "Effects of the Dynamite Charge," 642.

CHAPTER THREE

1. Franz Kafka, "Before the Law," *Franz Kafka: The Complete Stories and Parables* (1915; New York: Quality Paperback Book Club, 1971).

2. This has been extensively documented. See, e.g., Michelle Alexander, *The New Jim Crow* (New York: New Press, 2010); Angela Y. Davis, *Are Prisons Obsolete?* (New York: Seven Stories Press, 2005).

3. R. A. Duff, *Trials and Punishment* (Cambridge: Cambridge University Press, 1986).

4. Federal Judicial Center, accessed August 20, 2015, http://federalevidence.com/pdf/JuryInst/FJC_Crim_1987.pdf.

5. The current understanding of reasonable doubt was consolidated in the 1970 Supreme Court decision *re Winship* wherein the Court affirmed that the language of reasonable doubt was necessary for thinking about the burden that the state has to provide evidence for "every fact necessary to constitute the crime with which he is charged." In ruling on the case, which involved a juvenile being tried for a theft, the court found that the high standard of reasonable doubt was necessary, rather than the lower one of a preponderance of the evidence employed by the New York Family Court which had heard the case. The majority opinion delivered by Justice Brennan stated that the reasonable doubt standard played two essential functions in the criminal justice system: first, it is a "prime instrument for reducing the risk of convictions based on factual error." Second, "it is critical that the moral force of the criminal law not be diluted by a standard of proof that leave people in doubt whether innocent men are being condemned." It is interesting to note that the court focused on what the standard achieves rather than how it should be defined; in *re Winship* US 358 (1970).

6. Marianne Constable, *The Law of the Other: The Mixed Jury and Changing Conception of Citizenship, Law, and Knowledge* (Chicago: University of Chicago Press, 1993).

7. Constable, 147.

8. While the argument for radical enfranchisement does not hinge on a "collective wisdom" argument for the value of juries, it is apt in the case of assessing the motivations and credibility of witnesses. See, e.g., Hélène Landemore, "Democratic Reason: The Mechanism of Collective Intelligence in Politics," in *Collective Wisdom: Principles and Mechanisms*, ed. Hélène Landemore and Jon Elster (Cambridge: Cambridge University Press, 2012); James Surowiecki, *The Wisdom of Crowds* (New York: Anchor, 2005).

9. Francis Bacon, "A Proclamation for Jurors," in *The Works of Francis Bacon* (Cambridge: Cambridge University Press, 2011).

10. Bacon, 389.

11. John Locke, *An Essay Concerning Human Understanding* (Indianapolis, IN: Hackett, 1996).

12. Barbara J. Shapiro, *Beyond Reasonable Doubt and Probable Cause: Historical Perspectives on the Anglo-American Law of Evidence* (Berkeley: University of California Press, 1991), 13.

13. John Dewey, *How We Think* (Boston: D. C. Heath, 1910).

14. Daniel Kahneman, *Thinking Fast and Slow* (New York: Farrar, Straus, and Giroux, 2011).

15. Dewey, 101.

16. Samuel R. Sommers, "On Racial Diversity and Group Decision Making: Identifying Multiple Effects of Racial Composition on Jury Deliberations," *Journal of Personality and Social Psychology* 90 (2006): 597–612; "Determinants and Consequences of Jury Racial Diversity: Empirical Findings, Implications, and Directions for Future Research," *Social Issues and Policy Review* 2 (2008): 65–102.

17. Margaret C. Stevenson et al., "Racially Diverse Juries Promote Self-Monitoring Efforts During Jury Deliberation," *Translational Issues in Psychological Science* 3, no. 2 (2017): 187–201.

18. Stevenson et al.

19. Ralph Grunewald, "The Narrative of Innocence, or, Lost Stories," *Law and Literature* 25, no. 3 (2013): 375.

20. The Supreme Court considered the relevance of the presumption of innocence to those who are detained before trial in *Bell v. Wolfish*, 441 US 520, 533 (US 1979). In his dissent, Justice Marshall wrote, "Yet as the Court implicitly acknowledges, ante,

at 545, the rights of detainees, who have not been adjudicated guilty of a crime, are necessarily more extensive than those of prisoners 'who have been found to have violated one or more of the criminal laws established by society for its orderly governance.' Judicial tolerance of substantial impositions on detainees must be concomitantly less. However, by blindly deferring to administrative judgments on the rational basis for particular restrictions, the Court effectively delegates to detention officials the decision whether pretrial detainees have been punished. This, in my view, is an abdication of an unquestionably judicial function."

21. The Supreme Court has ruled that in voluntary discussions with the police, the right to not self-incriminate must be expressed explicitly; silence in response to questioning is not protected; *Salinas v. Texas*, 570 US (2013).

22. Richard Lippke, *Taming the Presumption of Innocence* (Oxford: Oxford University Press, 2016), 13.

23. For another approach, one that sees the value in drawing guilty inferences from the defendant's silence on the stand, see R. Kent Greenawalt, "Silence as a Moral and Constitutional Right," *William and Mary Law Review* 23, no. 1 (1981): 15–71.

24. David Dolinko, "Is There a Rationale for the Privilege against Self-Incrimination?," *UCLA Law Review* 33 (1985): 1064. Bentham also did not see anything cruel about being compelled to self-incriminate.

25. For an interesting take on the limits of the presumption of innocence for political life, see Lippke.

26. Martha Grace Duncan, "'So Young and So Untender': Remorseless Children and the Expectations of the Law," *Columbia Law Review* 102, no. 6 (2002): 1469–1526.

27. Sherman J. Clark, "The Juror, the Citizen, and the Human Being: The Presumption of Innocence and the Burden of Judgment," *Criminal Law and Philosophy* 8, no. 2 (2014): 421–29.

28. While an active presumption of innocence in the courtroom is a critical part of radical enfranchisement, its relationship to civic virtue is less direct. Duff has argued that an attitude of the presumption of innocence is desirable when it is translated to thinking about fellow citizens in the least negative way possible. We do not presume a stranger is innocent ("Innocent of what?" one might ask)—this would foreground their potential for criminal action in an undesirable way—but democracy would benefit, he says, from avoiding thinking of others as "enemies who might attack us. This modest truth shows itself in our demeanor as we walk down the street." R. A. Duff, "Who Must Presume Whom to Be Innocent of What?," *Netherlands Journal of Legal Philosophy* 42 (2013): 180.

29. For more on the story model, see Nancy Pennington and Reid Hastie, "Explaining the Evidence: Tests of the Story Model," *Journal of Personality and Social Psychology* 62, no. 2 (1992): 190.

30. For more on the qualities of narrative, see Jerome Bruner, "The Narrative Construction of Reality," *Critical Inquiry* 18, no. 1 (1981): 1–21.

31. Roland Barthes, *Mythologies*, trans. Annette Lavers (New York: Hill and Wang, 1972), 46.

32. For more on this, see Lisa Kern Griffin, "Narrative, Truth, and Trial," *Georgetown Law Journal* 101 (2013): 312.

33. Grunewald, "Narrative of Innocence," 380.

34. "And this raises the suspicion that narrative in general, from the folktale to the novel, from the annals to the fully realized 'history,' has to do with the topics of law, legality, legitimacy, or, more generally, authority. And indeed, when we look at what is

supposed to be the next stage in the evolution of historical representation after the annals form, that is, the chronicle, this suspicion is borne out. The more historically self-conscious the writer of any form of historiography, the more the question of the social system and the law which sustains it, the authority of this law and its justification, and threats to the law occupy his attention." Hayden White, "The Value of Narrativity in the Representation of Reality," *Critical Inquiry* 7, no. 1 (1980): 23.

35. For more on the impact of focusing on "when the trouble began" within legal narrative, see Kim Lane Scheppele, "Foreword: Telling Stories," *Michigan Law Review* 87, no. 8 (1989): 2073–98.

36. See also Sun Wolf, "Counterfactual Thinking in the Jury Room," *Small Group Research* 41, no. 4 (2010): 474–94.

37. White, "Value of Narrativity," 27.

38. On crime shows like "CSI" the forensic evidence, especially DNA evidence, often acts like the "smoking gun" that allows the viewer to decide a case definitively, but this television plot line acts as its own story narrative that makes it hard for real-life jurors to convict without such evidence.

39. Lisa Kerns Griffin shares these concerns about the dangers of a reliance on narrative and suggests a greater focus by the jury on evidence and logic as a counterweight to the subjective responses a compelling narrative elicits. Although I do not see an emphasis on objective evidence as the answer, I agree with her diagnosis of the problem. Lisa Kerns Griffin, "Narrative, Truth, and Trial." *Georgetown Law Journal* 101 (2013): 281–336.

40. *Bull*, a TV show that premiered on CBS in September, 2016, focuses on a jury consultant and tries to harness the dramatic potential of thinking about jurors as puppets to be manipulated by those who have the ability and resources to do so. Neil Genzlinger, "Michael Weatherly, Recast as Jury Puppeteer in 'Bull,'" *New York Times*, September 19, 2016.

41. Bruce B. Whitman, *The Inner Jury* (Philadelphia: Pine Street Press, 2014).

42. Whitman, 29.

43. Lynne Williams, "Anti-War Protestors and Civil Disobedience: A Tale of Two Juries," *Jury Expert* 26, no. 4 (2014): 22.

44. Griffin, "Narrative, Truth, and Trial," 330.

45. Griffin, "Narrative, Truth, and Trial," 328.

46. Sarah Koenig, host, *Serial* podcast, accessed August 10, 2015, www.serialpodcast.org.

47. Miranda Fricker, *Epistemic Injustice: Power and the Ethics of Knowing* (Oxford: Oxford University Press, 2007).

48. Fricker, 91.

49. Cynthia Lee, "Making Race Salient: Trayvon Martin and Implicit Bias in a Not yet Post-Racial Society," *North Carolina Law Review* 91 (2013): 1555–1612.

50. Experimental findings suggest that such attention to race will not, as some fear, lead to an overcorrection but rather outcomes that are more tied to the facts of the case and not the race of the defendant.

51. Peter A. Joy, "Race Matters in Jury Selection," *Northwestern University Law Review* 190 (2015): 180–86.

52. Mark W. Bennett, "Unraveling the Gordian Knot of Implicit Bias in Jury Selection: The Problems of Judge-Dominated Voir Dire, the Failed Promise of *Batson*, and Proposed Solutions," *Harvard Law and Policy Review* 4 (2010): 1207–29.

53. For a mock jury experiment that finds "debiasing instructions" given prior to the presentation of evidence effective in countering aversive racism, see Elizabeth

Ingriselli, "Mitigating Jurors' Racial Biases: The Effects of Content and Timing of Jury Instructions," *Yale Law Journal* 5 (2015): 1690–1745.

54. Bennett, "Unraveling the Gordian Knot," 169n.

CHAPTER FOUR

1. Dorothy Bailey, Bob Almond, and Kathleen Neumeyer, *Moral Uncertainty: Inside the Rodney King Juries* (United States: Andalou Books, 2017).

2. For an analysis of jury nullification from the perspective of recourse roles, that is a role in which rule departures occur only in specific circumstances, see Mortimer R. Kadish and Sanford H. Kadish, *Discretion to Disobey: A Study of Lawful Departures from Legal Rules* (Stanford, CA: Stanford University Press, 1973).

3. Akhil Reed Amar, *The Bill of Rights: Creation and Reconstruction* (New Haven, CT: Yale University Press, 2000).

4. Albert Dzur, "Democracy's "Free School": Tocqueville and Lieber on the Value of the Jury," *Political Theory* 38, no. 5 (2010): 603–30.

5. Dzur quotes Merton about the long-standing tensions between the lay and the professional in the courtroom. "Robert Merton claimed that ambivalence does not simply arise from professional malfeasance of lay people's suspicion that the professionals' interests are incongruent with their own but is a typical side effect of the long-term nature of lay-professional relations, the dependency involved, the asymmetry in authority, the fact that lay people can rarely judge the quality of professional work, and the fact that professionals are called in during times of trouble." Dzur, "Democracy's 'Free School,' " 617.

6. Philip Pettit, *Republicanism: A Theory of Freedom and Government* (Oxford: Oxford University Press 1999); Philip Pettit, *On the People's Terms: A Republican Theory and Model of Democracy* (Cambridge: Cambridge University Press, 2012); John P. McCormick, *Machiavellian Democracy* (Cambridge: Cambridge University Press, 2011).

7. For a critique of the republican solution as undermining the democratic value of election and the role of popular opinion, see Nadia Urbinati, "Unpolitical Democracy," *Political Theory* 38, no. 1 (2010): 65–92.

8. Pettit, *On the People's Terms*, 228.

9. John P. McCormick, "Subdue the Senate: Machiavelli's 'Way of Freedom' or Path to Tyranny?," *Political Theory* 40, no. 6 (2012): 728.

10. McCormick, *Machiavellian Democracy*, 108.

11. Melissa Schwartzberg, "The Ferocity of Hope: Accountability and the People's Tribunate in Machiavellian Democracy," *Good Society* 20, no. 2 (2011): 216–25.

12. Kadish and Kadish, *Discretion to Disobey*.

13. Kadish and Kadish, *Discretion to Disobey*, 60.

14. "The Institutionalization of Conflict: Jury Acquittals," in *Law, Justice, and the Individual in Society: Psychological and Legal Issues*, ed. June Louin Tapp and Felice J. Levine (New York: Holt, Rinehart, and Winston, 1977), 318.

15. Kadish and Kadish, *Discretion to Disobey*, 21.

16. Alex Tuckness and John M. Parrish, *The Decline of Mercy in Public Life* (Cambridge: Cambridge University Press, 2014).

17. US v. Dougherty, 154 US App. D.C. 76 (D.C. Cir. 1972).

18. The defendants were, however, granted a new trial on the grounds that they were denied self-representation.

19. Irwin A. Horowitz, Norbert L. Kerr, and Keith E. Niedermeier, "Jury Nullification: Legal and Psychological Perspectives," *Brooklyn Law Review* 66 (2001).

20. *US v. Dougherty*, 154 US App. D.C. 76 (D.C. Cir. 1972).
21. *US v. Dougherty*, 154 US App. D.C. 76 (D.C. Cir. 1972).
22. *US v. Thomas*, 116 US App (2nd Cir. 1997).
23. I am sympathetic to Brody's argument and the dangers of assuming that jurors always already know about the power to nullify. David C. Brody, "Sparf and Dougherty Revisited: Why the Court Should Instruct the Jury of Its Nullification Right," *American Criminal Law Review* 33, 89–122 (1995).
24. *US v. Thomas*, 116 F.3d 606 (2nd Cir. 1997)
25. *US v. Spock*, 416 F.2d 165 (1st Cir. 1969).
26. For an argument critical of special verdicts that is, in contrast, premised on a narrow understanding of juries only as triers of fact, see Jason Iuliano, "Jury Voting Paradoxes," *Michigan Law Review* 113, no. 3 (2015): 405–27. He argues that the discursive and lottery paradoxes that lead to a general verdict that may be inconsistent with the special verdict findings should give rise to reforms including conditional clauses on special verdict forms (to prevent internal inconsistencies) and a greater willingness by judges to redirect juries to examine their responses on special verdict forms such that their findings exhibit greater rationality within the closed system of the special verdict form.
27. *US v. Spock*, 416 F.2d 165 (1st Cir. 1969).
28. This point was prompted by Nepveu's defense of special verdicts and her call for adjustments in the language of special verdicts to ensure that they are not prejudicial against the defendant. Kate H. Nepveu, "Beyond 'Guilty' or 'Not Guilty': Giving Special Verdicts in Criminal Jury Trials," *Yale Law and Policy Review* 21 (2003): 263–300.
29. As in other reforms referenced here that may be consistent with radical enfranchisement, they will likely not be effective unless a larger transformation in the conceptions of jury service has occurred.
30. Nancy Marder, "The Myth of the Nullifying Jury," *Northwestern University Law Review* 93 (1999): 877–959; Clay S. Conrad, *Jury Nullification: The Evolution of a Doctrine* (Durham, NC: Carolina Academic Press, 1999); Jeffrey Abramson, *We, the Jury: The Jury System and the Ideal of Democracy* (Cambridge, MA: Harvard University Press, 2000); Brody, "Sparf and Dougherty Revisited."
31. Through an analysis of J. L. Borges's "The Lottery in Babylon," Barbara Goodwin suggested that greater randomization, via lotteries in many parts of public life, would be a powerful way to acknowledge and correct the systemic hierarchies of capitalist, liberal democracies. Barbara Goodwin, "Justice and the Lottery," in *Lotteries in Public Life*, ed. Peter Stone (1984; Charlottesville, VA: Imprint Academic, 2011).
32. Matthew R. Hall, "Guilty but Civilly Disobedient: Reconciling Civil Disobedience and the Rule of Law," *Cardoza Law Review* 28, no. 5 (2007): 2084.
33. See Alan W. Scheflin, "Jury Nullification: The Right to Say No," *Southern California Law Review* 45 (1972): 168–226.
34. For a revealing look at how prosecutorial misconduct is overlooked and buffered from sanction, making the intervention of a jury even more important, see Angela J. Davis, *Arbitrary Justice: The Power of the American Prosecutor* (Oxford: Oxford University Press, 2007).
35. Josiah Ober, "Relevant Expertise Aggregation: An Aristotelian Middle Way for Epistemic Democracy," *Princeton/Stanford Working Papers in Classics* (2012); Josiah Ober, *Democracy and Knowledge: Innovation and Learning in Classical Athens* (Princeton, NJ: Princeton University Press, 2008).
36. Ober, "Relevant Expertise Aggregation."

37. On collective wisdom, see also Hélène Landemore, "Democratic Reason: The Mechanism of Collective Intelligence in Politics," in *Collective Wisdom: Principles and Mechanisms*, ed. Hélène Landemore and Jon Elster (Cambridge: Cambridge University Press, 2012); James Surowiecki, *The Wisdom of Crowds* (New York: Anchor, 2005).

38. Josiah Ober, *Mass and Elite in Democratic Athens: Rhetoric, Ideology, and the Power of the People* (Princeton, NJ: Princeton University Press, 1990).

39. Paul Butler, "Racially Based Jury Nullification: Black Power in the Criminal Justice System," *Yale Law Journal* 105 (1995): 677–725.

40. It is interesting to think of Butler's prescription, alongside my own, in relation to the 1966 crisis strategy of Frances Fox Piven and Richard Cloward, who argued for enrollment in welfare programs by all those who were eligible in order to overwhelm the current system of benefits with the hope of establishing a guaranteed basic income.

41. Franklin E. Zimring, Gordon Hawkins, and Sam Kamin, *Punishment and Democracy: Three Strikes and You're Out in California* (New York: Oxford University Press, 2001); Kim Murphy, "Juries Are Giving Pot Defendants a Pass," *Los Angeles Times*, December 24, 2010.

42. Studies have shown that states that include jury notification about nullification as part of court procedure do not have higher acquittal rates; Brody, "Sparf and Dougherty Revisited."

43. R. A. Duff, *Punishment, Communication, and Community* (Oxford: Oxford University Press, 2003).

CHAPTER FIVE

1. Benjamin Weiser, "Trial by Jury, a Hallowed American Right, Is Vanishing," *New York Times*, August 7, 2016.

2. Plato, *Gorgias*, trans. Robin Waterfield (Oxford: Oxford University Press, 2008).

3. I. F. Stone, *The Trial of Socrates* (New York: Doubleday, 1989), 96.

4. Andrew Dilts, *Punishment and Inclusion: Race, Membership, and the Limits of American Liberalism* (New York: Fordham University Press, 2014), 88.

5. Keally McBride, *Law, Meaning, and Violence: Punishment and Political Order* (Ann Arbor: University of Michigan Press, 2009).

6. Michel Foucault, *Discipline and Punish: The Birth of the Prison* (New York: Pantheon Books, 1978).

7. Perry Zurn and Andrew Dilts, eds., *Active Intolerance: Michel Foucault, the Prison Information Group, and the Future of Abolition* (New York: Palgrave MacMillan, 2016).

8. R. A. Duff, *Punishment, Communication, and Community* (Oxford: Oxford University Press, 2003), 175.

9. Jenia Iontcheva, "Jury Sentencing as Democratic Practice," *Virginia Law Review* 89, no. 2 (2003); Albert Dzur, *Punishment, Participatory Democracy, and the Jury* (Oxford: Oxford University Press, 2012).

10. The empirical evidence on when a jury would be more punitive than a judge also gives me pause on this question. See Nancy King and Roosevelt Noble, "Jury Sentencing in Non-Capital Cases: Comparing Severity and Variance with Judicial Sentences in Two States," *Journal of Empirical Legal Studies* 2 (2005): 331–67.

11. Anthony Giacchino, *The Camden 28*, DVD, directed by Anthony Giacchino, New York: First Run Features (2007); Matt Zoller Seitz, "A Draft-Board Break-in That Put Activism on Trial," *New York Times*, July 27, 2007; Donald Janson, "Camden 28 Jury Asks Re-Reading," *New York Times*, May 19, 1973; Mark Edward Lender, *This*

Honorable Court: The United States District Court for the District of New Jersey, 1789–2000 (New Brunswick, NJ: Rutgers University Press, 2006).

12. Giacchino, *The Camden 28.*

13. Donald Janson, "FBI Is Accused of Aiding a Crime," *New York Times*, March 16, 1972; affidavit of Robert Hardy, County of Philadelphia, Commonwealth of Pennsylvania, February 28, 1972, accessed August 16, 2016, http://camden28.org/doc_picture11.htm.

14. Benjamin Weiser, "No Model Inmate, but Quite a Source; Once Incorrigible, an Informant Bonds with Terrorists," *New York Times*, July 25, 2003; Benjamin Weiser, "Former Assemblyman Turned Informer Avoids Prison," *New York Times*, September 11, 2014.

15. Tay Wiles, "The Jury for Key Bundy Trial in Las Vegas Has Been Selected," *High Country News*, November 2, 2017.

16. Kirk Siegler, "How the Bundy Trial Hits America's Widening Information Divide," November 16, 2017, npr.org.

17. Sarah Burns, *The Central Park Five: A Chronicle of City Wilding* (New York: Knopf, 2011).

18. Trisha Meili, *I Am the Central Park Jogger: A Story of Hope and Possibility* (New York: Scribner, 2003).

19. Benjamin Weiser, "5 Exonerated in Central Park Jogger Case Agree to Settle Suit for $40 Million," *New York Times*, June 19, 2014.

20. Joan Didion, "New York: Sentimental Journeys," *New York Review of Books* (January 17, 1991).

21. Harold Brueland, "The Juror's Story," *Daily News*, republished April 9, 2013.

22. Brueland.

23. See, e.g., *Frazier v. Cupp*, 394 US 731(1969) where the Supreme Court affirmed the use of deceptive interrogation tactics and allowed a confession to be considered valid even when the defendant was falsely told that his cosuspect had confessed.

24. Peter Brooks, *Troubling Confessions: Speaking Guilt in Law and Literature* (Chicago: University of Chicago Press, 2000), 11.

25. For a description of how police officers are encouraged to conduct interrogations in light of the Reid technique, see Brooks, 39.

26. Fred E. Inbau et al., *Essentials of the Reid Technique: Criminal Interrogation and Confessions* (Burlington, MA: Jones and Bartlett Learning, 2014).

27. Despite the stronghold that the prosecution's story had on the media, a group of reporters and city officials known as The Group met to talk about the troubling implications of the media coverage. LynNell Hancock, "Wolf Pack: The Press and the Central Park Jogger," *Columbia Journalism Review* (January/February 2003): 39.

28. Saul Kassin, "The Social Psychology of False Confessions," *Social Issues and Policy Review* 9, no. 1 (2015): 25–51.

29. This type of false confession fits with what Wrightsman and Kassin call "coerced-compliant" confessions where defendants confess to escape harsh interrogation. This is distinguished from the voluntary false confessions made in the aftermath of a publicized crime or those made in the rare event that the defendant comes to believe she has, in fact, committed the crime; Kassin.

30. Saul M. Kassin, Christian A. Meissner, and Rebecca J. Norwick, "I'd Know a False Confession If I Saw One: A Comparative Study of College Students and Police Investigators," *Law and Human Behavior* 29, no. 2 (2005): 211–27.

31. Ronald Sullivan, "Defense Calls Jogger Case a Racist Witch Hunt," *New York Times*, November 29, 1990.

32. Alice Cantwell, Joseph McNamara, and Maria Mooshil, "2 Found Guilty in Jog Case," *Daily News*, Central Park Five Archive, December 12, 1990 (updated April 9, 2013).

33. Kassin, "Social Psychology," 44.

34. James C. McKinley Jr., "Woman Found Guilty of Assaulting Officer at an Occupy Wall Street Protest," *New York Times*, May 5, 2014; Todd Gitlin, "Cecily McMillan from Zuccotti Park to Rikers," *New Yorker* (May 23, 2014).

35. Jon Swaine, "Cecily McMillan Jurors Tell Judge Occupy Activist Should Not Go to Jail," *Guardian*, May 8, 2014.

36. Swaine.

37. See Dzur, *Punishment, Participatory Democracy, and the Jury*; Iontcheva, "Jury Sentencing as Democratic Practice."

38. See the discussion in Darryl K. Brown, "Jury Nullification within the Rule of Law." *Minnesota Law Review* 81, no. 5 (May 1997).

39. Scott Shane, "Obama Takes a Hard Line against Leaks to Press," *New York Times*, June 11, 2010.

40. Spencer Ackerman and Ed Pilkington, "Obama's War on Whistleblowers Leaves Administration Insiders Unscathed," *Guardian*, March 16, 2015.

41. Glenn Greenwald, "Kiriakou and Stuxnet: The Danger of the Still-Escalating Obama Whistleblower War," *Guardian*, January 27, 2013; Scott Shane, "Ex-Officer Is First from C.I.A. to Face Prison for a Leak," *New York Times*, January 5, 2013.

42. Peter Finn and Sari Horwitz, "US Charges Snowden with Espionage," *Washington Post*, June 21, 2013.

43. On his desire to make a presentation to a jury, Snowden said, "Daniel Ellsberg himself has argued that I made the right decision not to present myself to the court. Things have changed since the 1970's, and today the law doesn't allow you to make a defense against Espionage Act charges in front of the jury. I am legally prohibited from even speaking to the jury about my motivation. Can there be a fair trial when you can't put forward a defense? At the sentencing phase you can express to the judge why you did what you did, but that is not democratic. The jury system was created so you can discuss with your peers what you did, why you did it." Steven Erlanger, "Edward Snowden: Do I Think Things are Fixed? No," *New York Times*, December 7, 2016.

44. Emma Goldman, "Prisons: A Social Crime and Failure," in *Anarchism and Other Essays* (New York: Mother Earth Publishing Association, 1911).

BIBLIOGRAPHY

Abramson, Jeffrey. *We, the Jury: The Jury System and the Ideal of Democracy*. Cambridge, MA: Harvard University Press, 2000.

Ackerman, Spencer, and Ed Pilkington. "Obama's War on Whistleblowers Leaves Administration Insiders Unscathed." *Guardian* (March 16, 2015).

Alexander, Michelle. *The New Jim Crow*. New York: New Press, 2010.

Alschuler, Albert W. "Plea Bargaining and Its History." *Columbia Law Review* 79, no. 1 (1979): 1–43.

Amar, Akhil Reed. *The Bill of Rights: Creation and Reconstruction* New Haven, CT: Yale University Press, 2000.

———. "Reinventing Juries: Ten Suggested Reforms." *UC Davis Law Review* 28(1995): 1169–94.

American Bar Association. "The Allen Charge Dilemma." *American Criminal Law Review* 10 (1972): 637.

Bacon, Francis. "A Proclamation for Jurors." In *The Works of Francis Bacon*. Cambridge: Cambridge University Press, 2011.

Bailey, Dorothy, Bob Almond, and Kathleen Neumeyer. *Moral Uncertainty: Inside the Rodney King Juries*. United States: Andalou Books, 2017.

Barthes, Roland. *Mythologies*. Translated by Annette Lavers. New York: Hill and Wang, 1972.

Benhabib, Seyla. *Situating the Self*. Cambridge: Polity Press, 1992.

Bennett, Mark W. "Unraveling the Gordian Knot of Implicit Bias in Jury Selection: The Problems of Judge-Dominated Voir Dire, the Failed Promise of *Batson*, and Proposed Solutions." *Harvard Law and Policy Review* 4 (2010): 1207–29.

Bohman, James. "Critical Theory and Democracy." In *Handbook of Critical Theory*, edited by David M. Rasmussen. Oxford: Blackwell, 1996.

———. "'System' and 'Lifeworld': Habermas and the Problem of Holism." *Philosophy and Social Criticism* 15 (1989): 381–401.

Brody, David C. "Sparf and Dougherty Revisited: Why the Court Should Instruct the Jury of Its Nullification Right." *American Criminal Law Review* 33 (1995): 89–122.

Brooks, Peter. *Troubling Confessions: Speaking Guilt in Law and Literature*. Chicago: University of Chicago Press, 2000.

Brown, Darryl K. "Jury Nullification within the Rule of Law." *Minnesota Law Review* 81, no. 5 (May 1997): 1149–200.

Brueland, Harold. "The Juror's Story." *Daily News*, republished April 9, 2013.

Bruner, Jerome. "The Narrative Construction of Reality." *Critical Inquiry* 18, no. 1 (1981): 1–21.

Burnett, D. Graham. *A Trial by Jury*. New York: Alfred A. Knopf, 2001.

Burns, Robert P. *The Death of the American Trial*. Chicago: University of Chicago Press, 2009.

———. *A Theory of the Trial*. Princeton, NJ: Princeton University Press, 1999.

Burns, Sarah. *The Central Park Five: A Chronicle of City Wilding*. New York: Knopf, 2011.

Butler, Judith. "Endangered/Endangering: Schematic Racism and White Paranoia." In *Reading Rodney King/Reading Urban Uprising*, edited by Robert Gooding-Williams. New York: Routledge, 1993.

Butler, Paul. "Racially Based Jury Nullification: Black Power in the Criminal Justice System." *Yale Law Journal* 105 (1995): 677–725.

Canovan, Margaret. *Populism*. New York: Houghton Mifflin Harcourt, 1981.

Chambers, Simone. "Discourse and Democratic Practices." In *Cambridge Companion to Habermas*, edited by Stephen K. White. Cambridge: Cambridge University Press, 2006.

Chesterton, G. K. "The Twelve Men." In *Tremendous Trifles*. New York: Dodd, Mead, 1920.

Clark, Sherman J. "The Juror, the Citizen, and the Human Being: The Presumption of Innocence and the Burden of Judgment." *Criminal Law and Philosophy* 8, no. 2 (2014): 421–29.

Conrad, Clay S. *Jury Nullification: The Evolution of a Doctrine*. Durham, NC: Carolina Academic Press, 1999.

Constable, Marianne. *The Law of the Other: The Mixed Jury and Changing Conception of Citizenship, Law, and Knowledge*. Chicago: University of Chicago Press, 1993.

Coughlan, Peter J. "In Defense of Unanimous Jury Verdicts: Mistrials, Communication, and Strategic Voting." *American Political Science Review* 94, no. 2 (2000): 375–93.

Cover, Robert. "Violence and the Word." *Yale Law Journal* 95 (1986): 1601–31.

Davis, Angela J. *Arbitrary Justice: The Power of the American Prosecutor*. Oxford: Oxford University Press, 2007.

Davis, Angela Y. *Are Prisons Obsolete?* New York: Seven Stories Press, 2005.

Delaune, Tim. "Democratizing the Criminal: Jury Nullification as Exercise of Sovereign Discretion over the Friend-Enemy Distinction." PhD diss., University of Massachusetts, Amherst, 2013.

Devine, Dennis D. *Jury Decision-Making: The State of the Science*. New York: NYU Press, 2012.

Dewey, John. *How We Think*. Boston: D. C. Heath, 1910.

Didion, Joan. "New York: Sentimental Journeys." *New York Review of Books* (January 17, 1991).

Dilts, Andrew. *Punishment and Inclusion: Race, Membership and the Limits of American Liberalism*. New York: Fordham University Press, 2014.

Dolinko, David. "Is There a Rationale for the Privilege against Self-Incrimination?" *UCLA Law Review* 33 (1985): 1063–148.

Duff, R. A. "Who Must Presume Whom to Be Innocent of What?" *Netherlands Journal of Legal Philosophy* 42 (2013): 170–92.

———. Lindsay Farmer, Sandra Marshall, and Victor Tadros. *The Trial on Trial: Towards a Normative Theory of the Criminal Trial*. London: Bloomsbury, 2007.

———. *Punishment, Communication, and Community*. Oxford: Oxford University Press, 2003.

———. *Trials and Punishment*. Cambridge: Cambridge University Press, 1986.

Duncan, Martha Grace. "'So Young and So Untender': Remorseless Children and the Expectations of the Law." *Columbia Law Review* 102, no. 6 (2002): 1469–526.

Dworkin, R. M. "Is Law a System of Rules?" In *The Philosophy of Law*, edited by R. M. Dworkin. Oxford: Oxford University Press, 1977.

Dzur, Albert. "Democracy's 'Free School': Tocqueville and Lieber on the Value of the Jury." *Political Theory* 38, no. 5 (2010): 603–30.

———. "The Myth of Penal Populism." *Journal of Speculative Philosophy* 24, no. 4 (2010): 354–75.

———. *Punishment, Participatory Democracy, and the Jury*. Oxford: Oxford University Press, 2012.

Dzur, Albert, Ian Loader, and Richard Sparks, eds. *Democratic Theory and Mass Incarceration*. New York: Oxford University Press, 2016.

Dzur, Albert W., and Rekha Mirchandani. "Punishment and Democracy: The Role of Public Deliberation." *Punishment and Society* 9 (2007): 151–75.

Ferguson, Andrew Guthrie. *Why Jury Duty Matters*. New York: NYU Press, 2012.

Finkel, Norman J. *Commonsense Justice: Jurors' Notions of the Law*. Cambridge, MA: Harvard University Press, 2009.

Finn, Peter, and Sari Horwitz. "U.S. Charges Snowden with Espionage." *Washington Post* (June 21, 2013).

Forman, James, Jr. *Locking up Our Own: Crime and Punishment in Black America*. New York: Farrar, Straus, and Giroux, 2017.

Foucault, Michel. *Discipline and Punish: The Birth of the Prison*. New York: Pantheon Books, 1978.

Frank, Jason. *Constituent Moments: Enacting the People in Postrevolutionary America*. Durham, NC: Duke University Press, 2009.

Fraser, Nancy. "Rethinking the Public Sphere: A Contribution to the Critique of Actually Existing Democracy." In *Habermas and the Public Sphere*, edited by Craig Calhoun. Cambridge: MIT Press, 1992.

Fricker, Miranda. *Epistemic Injustice: Power and the Ethics of Knowing*. Oxford: Oxford University Press, 2007.

Gastil, John, E. Pierre Deess, Philip J. Weiser, and Cindy Simmons. *The Jury and Democracy: How Jury Deliberation Promotes Civic Engagement and Political Participation*. New York: Oxford University Press, 2010.

Giacchino, Anthony. *The Camden 28* (DVD). Directed by Anthony Giacchino, New York: First Run Features (2007).

Gitlin, Todd. "Cecily McMillan from Zuccotti Park to Rikers." *New Yorker* (May 23, 2014).

Goldman, Emma. "Prisons: A Social Crime and Failure." In *Anarchism and Other Essays*, 115–32. New York: Mother Earth Publishing Association, 1911.

Goodwin, Barbara. "Justice and the Lottery." In *Lotteries in Public Life*, edited by Peter Stone. Charlottesville, VA: Imprint Academic, 2011 (1984).

Gottschalk, Marie. *Caught: The Prison State and the Lockdown of American Politics*. Princeton, NJ: Princeton University Press, 2016.

Greenawalt, R. Kent. "Silence as a Moral and Constitutional Right." *William and Mary Law Review* 23, no. 1 (1981): 15–71.

Greenwald, Glenn. "Kiriakou and Stuxnet: The Danger of the Still-Escalating Obama Whistleblower War." *Guardian*, January 27, 2013.

Gregg, Pauline. *Free-Born John: A Biography of John Lilburne*. London: Harrap, 1961.

Griffin, Lisa Kern. "Narrative, Truth, and Trial." *Georgetown Law Journal* 101 (2013): 281–336.

Grunewald, Ralph. "The Narrative of Innocence, or, Lost Stories." *Law and Literature* 25, no. 3 (2013): 366–89.

Guttman, Amy. *Democratic Education*. Princeton, NJ: Princeton University Press, 1999.

Habermas, Jürgen. *Between Facts and Norms: Contributions to a Discourse Theory of Law and Democracy*. Cambridge, MA: MIT Press, 1998.

———. "Civil Disobedience: Litmus Test for the Democratic Constitutional State." *Berkeley Journal of Sociology* 30 (1985): 95–116.

———. *Moral Consciousness and Communicative Action*. Cambridge, MA: MIT Press, 2001.

Hale, Dennis. *The Jury in America: Triumph and Decline*. Lawrence: University Press of Kansas, 2016.

Hall, Matthew R. "Guilty but Civilly Disobedient: Reconciling Civil Disobedience and the Rule of Law." *Cardoza Law Review* 28, no. 5 (2007): 2083–169.

Hancock, LynNell. "Wolf Pack: The Press and the Central Park Jogger." *Columbia Journalism Review* (January/February 2003).

Harcourt, Bernard. "Abolition in the U.S.A. by 2050: On Political Capital and Ordinary Acts of Resistance." In *Road to Abolition?*, edited by Austin Sarat and Charles Ogletree. New York: NYU Press, 2009.

Hobbes, Thomas. *Leviathan*. Indianapolis, IN: Hackett, 1994.

Honoré, Tony. *Ulpian*. Oxford: Oxford University Press, 1982.

Horowitz, Irwin A., Norbert L. Kerr, and Keith E. Niedermeier. "Jury Nullification: Legal and Psychological Perspectives." *Brooklyn Law Review* 66 (2001): 1207–49.

Howe, Mark Dewolfe. "Juries as Judges of Criminal Law." *Harvard Law Review* 52, no. 582 (1939): 613–48.

Inbau, Fred E., John E. Reid, Joseph P. Buckley, and Brian C. Jayne. *Essentials of the Reid Technique: Criminal Interrogation and Confessions*. Burlington, MA: Jones and Bartlett Learning, 2014.

Ingriselli, Elizabeth. "Mitigating Jurors' Racial Biases: The Effects of Content and Timing of Jury Instructions." *Yale Law Journal* 5 (2015): 1690–1745.

Iontcheva, Jenia. "Jury Sentencing as Democratic Practice." *Virginia Law Review* 89, no. 2 (2003): 311–81.

Iuliano, Jason. "Jury Voting Paradoxes." *Michigan Law Review* 113, no. 3 (2015): 405–27.

Jacobsohn, Gary J. "The Right to Disagree: Judges, Juries, and the Administration of Criminal Justice in Maryland." *Washington University Law Review* 4 (1976): 571–607.

———. "The Unanimous Verdict: Politics and the Jury Trial." *Washington University Law Quarterly* 39 (1977): 39–57.

Janara, Laura. "Democracy's Family Values." In *Feminist Interpretations of Alexis De Tocqueville*, edited by Jill Locke and Eileen Hunt Botting. University Park, PA: Penn State University Press, 2008.

Janson, Donald. "Camden 28 Jury Asks Re-Reading." *New York Times*, May 19, 1973.

Johnson, Sheri. "Black Innocence and the White Jury." *Michigan Law Review* 83, no. 7 (1985): 1611–1707.

Jonakait, Randolph N. *The American Jury System*. New Haven, CT: Yale University Press, 2003.

Joy, Peter A. "Race Matters in Jury Selection." *Northwestern University Law Review* 190, no. 80 (2015): 180–86.

Kadish, Mortimer R., and Sanford H. Kadish. *Discretion to Disobey: A Study of Lawful Departures from Legal Rules*. Stanford, CA: Stanford University Press, 1973.

———. "The Institutionalization of Conflict: Jury Acquittals." In *Law, Justice and the Individual in Society: Psychological and Legal Issues*, edited by June Louin Tapp and Felice J. Levine. New York: Holt, Rinehart, and Winston, 1977.

Kahneman, Daniel. *Thinking Fast and Slow*. New York: Farrar, Straus, and Giroux, 2011.

Kalven, Harry, and Hans Zeisel. *The American Jury*. Chicago: University of Chicago Press, 1971.

Kaplan, Martin F., and Charles E. Miller. "Group Decision Making and Normative Versus Informational Influence: Effects of Type of Issue and Assigned Decision Rule." *Journal of Personality and Social Psychology* 53, no. 2 (1987): 306–13.

Kassin, Saul. "The Social Psychology of False Confessions." *Social Issues and Policy Review* 9, no. 1 (2015): 25–51.

Kassin, Saul M., Christian A. Meissner, and Rebecca J. Norwick. "I'd Know a False Confession If I Saw One: A Comparative Study of College Students and Police Investigators." *Law and Human Behavior* 29, no. 2 (2005): 211–27.

King, Nancy, and Roosevelt Noble. "Jury Sentencing in Non-Capital Cases: Comparing Severity and Variance with Judicial Sentences in Two States." *Journal of Empirical Legal Studies* 2 (2005): 331–67.

Kleinfeld, Joshua. "Two Cultures of Punishment." *Stanford Law Review* 68, no. 5 (2016): 933–1037.

Kramer, Larry D. *The People Themselves: Popular Constitutionalism and Judicial Review*. New York: Oxford University Press 2004.

Krauss, Stanton D. "An Inquiry into the Right of Criminal Juries to Determine the Law in Colonial America." *Journal of Criminal Law and Criminology* 89 (1998): 111–213.

Landemore, Hélène. "Democratic Reason: The Mechanism of Collective Intelligence in Politics." In *Collective Wisdom: Principles and Mechanisms*, edited by Hélène Landemore and Jon Elster. Cambridge: Cambridge University Press, 2012.

———. *Democratic Reason: Politics, Collective Intelligence, and the Rule of the Many*. Princeton, NJ: Princeton University Press, 2013.

Lanier, Mark, and Cloud Miller III. "The Allen Charge: Expedient Justice or Coercion?" *American Journal of Criminal Justice* 25, no. 1 (2000): 31–40.

Lee, Cynthia. "Making Race Salient: Trayvon Martin and Implicit Bias in a Not Yet Post-Racial Society." *North Carolina Law Review* 91 (2013): 1555–1612.

Lender, Mark Edward. *This Honorable Court: The United States District Court for the District of New Jersey, 1789–2000*. New Brunswick, NJ: Rutgers University Press, 2006.

Lippke, Richard. *Taming the Presumption of Innocence*. Oxford: Oxford University Press, 2016.

Locke, John. *An Essay Concerning Human Understanding*. Indianapolis, IN: Hackett, 1996.

MacIntyre, Alasdair. *After Virtue*. South Bend, IN: University of Notre Dame Press, 1981.

Marder, Nancy. *The Jury Process*. New York: Foundation Press, 2005.

———. "The Myth of the Nullifying Jury." *Northwestern University Law Review* 93 (1999): 877–959.

Maxwell, Lida. *Public Trials: Burke, Zola, and Arendt on the Politics of Lost Causes*. New York: Oxford University Press, 2015.

McBride, Keally. *Law, Meaning, and Violence: Punishment and Political Order*. Ann Arbor: University of Michigan Press, 2009.

McConville, Mike, and Chester L. Mirsky. *Jury Trials and Plea Bargaining: A True History*. London: Hart Publishing, 2005.

McCormick, John P. *Machiavellian Democracy*. Cambridge: Cambridge University Press, 2011.

———. "Subdue the Senate: Machiavelli's 'Way of Freedom' or Path to Tyranny?" *Political Theory* 40, no. 6 (2012): 714–35.

McKinley, James C., Jr. "Woman Found Guilty of Assaulting Officer at an Occupy Wall Street Protest." *New York Times*, May 5, 2014.

Meili, Trisha. *I Am the Central Park Jogger: A Story of Hope and Possibility*. New York: Scribner, 2003.

Meyer, Linda Ross. "The Merciful State." In *Forgiveness, Mercy, and Clemency*, edited by Austin Sarat and Nasser Hussain. Stanford, CA: Stanford University Press, 2007.

Moon, J. Donald. "Practical Discourse and Communicative Ethics." In *Cambidge Companion to Habermas*, edited by Stephen K. White. Cambridge: Cambridge University Press, 2006.

Muller, Jan-Werner. *What Is Populism?* Philadelphia: University of Pennsylvania Press, 2016.

Murphy, Andrew. "Trial Transcript as Political Theory: Principles and Performance in the Penn-Mead Case." *Political Theory* 41, no. 6 (2013): 775–808.

Murphy, Kim. "Juries Are Giving Pot Defendants a Pass." *Los Angeles Times*, December 24, 2010.

Nepveu, Kate H. "Beyond 'Guilty' or 'Not Guilty': Giving Special Verdicts in Criminal Jury Trials." *Yale Law and Policy Review* 21 (2003): 263–300.

Ober, Josiah. *Democracy and Knowledge: Innovation and Learning in Classical Athens*. Princeton, NJ: Princeton University Press, 2008.

———. *Mass and Elite in Democratic Athens: Rhetoric, Ideology, and the Power of the People*. Princeton, NJ: Princeton University Press, 1990.

———. "Relevant Expertise Aggregation: An Aristotelian Middle Way for Epistemic Democracy." *Princeton/Stanford Working Papers in Classics* (2012).

Pennington, Nancy, and Reid Hastie. "Explaining the Evidence: Tests of the Story Model." *Journal of Personality and Social Psychology* 62, no. 2 (1992): 189–206.

Pettit, Philip. "Is Criminal Justice Politically Feasible?" *Buffalo Criminal Law Review* 5, no. 2 (2002): 427–50.

———. *On the People's Terms: A Republican Theory and Model of Democracy*. Cambridge: Cambridge University Press, 2012.

———. *Republicanism: A Theory of Freedom and Government*. Oxford: Oxford University Press, 1999.

Plato. *Gorgias*. Translated by Robin Waterfield. Oxford: Oxford University Press.

Pratt, John. *Penal Populism*. London: Routledge, 2008.

Rancière, Jacques. *Dissensus: On Politics and Aesthetics*. London: Continuum International Publishing Group, 2010.

Rehg, William. "Habermas's Discourse Theory of Law and Democracy: An Overview of the Argument." In *Handbook of Critical Theory*, edited by David M. Rasmussen. Oxford: Blackwell, 1996.

Rescher, Nicholas. *Pluralism: Against the Demand for Consensus*. Oxford: Oxford University Press, 1995.

Reznik, Judith. "Migrating, Morphing, and Vanishing: The Empirical and Normative Puzzles of Declining Trial Rates in Court." *Journal of Empirical Legal Studies* 1, no. 3 (2004): 783–841.

Robinson, Paul H., and John M. Darley. *Justice, Liability and Blame: Community Views and the Criminal Law*. Boulder, CO: Westview Press, 1995.

Roots, Roger. "The Rise and Fall of the American Jury." *Seton Hall Circuit Review* 8, no. 1(2011): 1–42.

Rosenfeld, Sophia. *Common Sense: A Political History*. Cambridge, MA: Harvard University Press, 2011.

Saks, Michael. "The Smaller the Jury, the Greater the Unpredictability." *Judicature* 79 (1996): 263–65.

Sanders, Lynn. "Against Deliberation." *Political Theory* 25, no. 3 (1997): 347–76.

Scheflin, Alan W. "Jury Nullification: The Right to Say No." *Southern California Law Review* 45 (1972): 168–226.

Scheppele, Kim Lane. "Foreword: Telling Stories." *Michigan Law Review* 87, no. 8 (1989): 2073–98.

Schmitt, Carl. *The Concept of the Political*. Chicago: University of Chicago Press, 1996.

Schwan, Christopher C. "Right up to the Line: The Ethics of Advancing Nullification Arguments to the Jury." *Journal of the Legal Profession* 29 (2004–5): 293–304.

Schwartz, Edward P., and Warren F. Schwartz. "Decisionmaking by Juries under Unanimity and Supermajority Voting Rules." *Georgetown Law Journal* 80 (1991–92): 775–808.

Schwartzberg, Melissa. *Counting the Many: The Origins and Limits of Supermajority Rule*. New York: Cambridge University Press, 2014.

———. "The Ferocity of Hope: Accountability and the People's Tribunate in Machiavellian Democracy." *Good Society* 20, no. 2 (2011): 216–25.

Seitz, Matt Zoller. "A Draft-Board Break-in That Put Activism on Trial." *New York Times*, July 27, 2007.

Shane, Scott. "Ex-Officer Is First from C.I.A. To Face Prison for a Leak." *New York Times*, January 5, 2013.

———. "Obama Takes a Hard Line against Leaks to Press." *New York Times*, June 11, 2010.

Shapiro, Barbara J. *Beyond Reasonable Doubt and Probable Cause: Historical Perspectives on the Anglo-American Law of Evidence*. Berkeley: University of California Press, 1991.

Shklar, Judith. "Political Theory and Rule of Law." In *Political Thought and Political Thinkers*. Chicago: University of Chicago Press, 1998.

Siegler, Kirk. "How the Bundy Trial Hits America's Widening Information Divide." *npr.org*, November 16, 2017.

Simon, Jonathan. *Governing through Crime*. New York: Oxford University Press, 2007.

Smith, Vicki L., and Saul M. Kassin. "Effects of the Dynamite Charge on the Deliberations of Deadlocked Mock Juries." *Law and Human Behavior* 17, no. 6 (1993): 625–43.

Sommers, Samuel R. "Determinants and Consequences of Jury Racial Diversity: Empirical Findings, Implications, and Directions for Future Research." *Social Issues and Policy Review* 2 (2008): 65–102.

———. "On Racial Diversity and Group Decision Making: Identifying Multiple Effects of Racial Composition on Jury Deliberations." *Journal of Personality and Social Psychology* 90 (2006): 597–612.

Spooner, Lysander. *An Essay on the Trial by Jury*. Boston: John P. Jewett and Company, 1852.

Stevenson, Margaret C., Brad L. Lytle, BreighAnna J. Baumholser, and Evan W. McCracken. "Racially Diverse Juries Promote Self-Monitoring Efforts During Jury Deliberation." *Translational Issues in Psychological Science* 3, no. 2 (2017): 187–201.

Stimson, Shannon. *The American Revolution in the Law: Anglo-American Jurisprudence before John Marshall*. Princeton, NJ: Princeton University Press, 1990.

Stone, I. F. *The Trial of Socrates*. New York: Doubleday, 1989.

Stone, Peter. *Lotteries in Public Life*. Charlottesville, VA: Imprint Academic, 2011.

Sullivan, Ronald. "Defense Calls Jogger Case a Racist Witch Hunt." *New York Times*, November 29, 1990.

Sundby, Scott E. *A Life and Death Decision: A Jury Weighs the Death Penalty*. New York: St. Martin Griffin, 2005.

Surowiecki, James. *The Wisdom of Crowds*. New York: Anchor, 2005.

Swaine, Jon. "Cecily McMillan Jurors Tell Judge Occupy Activist Should Not Go to Jail." *Guardian*, May 8, 2014.

Thomassen, Lasse. "Communicative Reason, Deconstruction and Foundationalism: A Response to White and Farr." *Political Theory* 41, no. 3 (2013): 482–88.

Tocqueville, Alexis de. *Democracy in America*. Edited by Harvey C. Mansfield and Debra Winthrop. Chicago: University of Chicago Press, 2000.

———. *The Old Regime and the Revolution*. Chicago: University of Chicago Press, 1998.

Tuck, Richard. "Hobbes and the Jury." Unpublished Work (2011).

Tuckness, Alex, and John M. Parrish. *The Decline of Mercy in Public Life*. Cambridge: Cambridge University Press, 2014.

Umphrey, Martha Merrill. "Fragile Performances: The Dialogics of Judgment in a Theory of the Trial." *Law and Social Inquiry* 28, no. 2 (2003): 527–32.

Urbinati, Nadia. "Unpolitical Democracy." *Political Theory* 38, no. 1 (2010): 65–92.

Vidmar, Neil, and Valerie P. Hans. *American Juries: The Verdict*. Amherst, NY: Prometheus Books, 2007.

Weiser, Benjamin. "Five Exonerated in Central Park Jogger Case Agree to Settle Suit for $40 Million." *New York Times*, June 19, 2014.

———. "Former Assemblyman Turned Informer Avoids Prison." *New York Times*, September 11, 2014.

———. "No Model Inmate, but Quite a Source; Once Incorrigible, an Informant Bonds with Terrorists." *New York Times*, July 25, 2003.

———. "Trial by Jury, a Hallowed American Right, Is Vanishing." *New York Times*, August 7, 2016.

Wellmer, Allbrecht. "Ethics and Dialogue." Translated by David Midgley. In *The Persistence of Modernity: Essays on Aesthetics, Ethics and Postmodernism*. Cambridge: Polity Press, 1991.

White, Hayden. "The Value of Narrativity in the Representation of Reality." *Critical Inquiry* 7, no. 1 (1980): 5–27.

White, Stephen K. *Recent Work of Jürgen Habermas: Reason, Justice and Modernity*. Cambridge: Cambridge University Press, 1988.

White, Stephen K., and Evan Robert Farr. "'No-Saying' in Habermas." *Political Theory* 40, no. 1 (2012): 32–57.

Whitman, Bruce B. *The Inner Jury*. Philadelphia: Pine Street Press, 2014.

Whitman, James Q. "What Happened to Tocqueville's America?" *Social Research* 74, no. 2 (2007): 251–68.

Wiles, Tay. "The Jury for Key Bundy Trial in Las Vegas Has Been Selected." *High Country News*, November 2, 2017.

Williams, Lynne. "Anti-War Protestors and Civil Disobedience: A Tale of Two Juries." *Jury Expert* 26, no. 4 (2014): 1–4.

Winthrop, Delba. "Tocqueville's American Woman and 'the True Conception of Democratic Progress.'" *Political Theory* 14, no. 2 (1986): 239–61.

Wolf, Sun. "Counterfactual Thinking in the Jury Room." *Small Group Research* 41, no. 4 (2010): 474–94.

Wolin, Sheldon. "Fugitive Democracy." *Constellations* 1, no. 1 (1994): 11–25.

———. *Tocqueville between Two Worlds: The Making of a Political and Theoretical Life*. Princeton, NJ: Princeton University Press.

Young, Iris Marion. "Impartiality and the Civic Public: Some Implications of Feminist Critiques of Moral and Political Theory." *Praxis International* 5, no. 4 (1986): 381–401.

Zimring, Franklin E., Gordon Hawkins, and Sam Kamin. *Punishment and Democracy: Three Strikes and You're Out in California*. New York: Oxford University Press, 2001.

Zurn, Perry, and Andrew Dilts, eds. *Active Intolerance: Michel Foucault, the Prison Information Group, and the Future of Abolition*. New York: Palgrave MacMillan, 2016.

INDEX

Abramson, Jeffery, 93
African Americans, 82; criminal justice system, 62; and incarceration, 16; punitive sentencing, 95; systematic bias against, 95; three-option verdict, 96
Allen Charge, 40–42, 44, 47–50, 52, 54, 57, 59, 123n1; belief, language of, 56; unanimity, ideal of, 58
Altschuler, Albert, 10
American Revolution, 31
Anglo-American legal thought, 86
anti-Federalists, 31
Apodaca v. Oregon, 46
Aristotle, 15, 121n50
Asia, 88
Athens, 95; Athenian model, 94, 97, 100–101

Bacon, Francis, 66
Barthes, Roland, 73; and doxa, 18
Batson v. Kentucky, 15, 79, 119n19
Bazelon, Emily, 90
Beccaria, Cesare, 99
Before the Law (Kafka), 61
Bell v. Wolfish, 127–28n20
Bennett, Mark, 79–80
Bentham, Jeremy, 128n24
bias: as implicit, 62, 114; and judges, 104; and jurors, 62, 71, 73, 109; jury selection, 79; and presentation, 79; racist attitudes, 80; as unconscious, and racial stereotypes, 78
Bill of Rights, 37
Borges, J. L., 131n31

Brennan, William J. Jr., 127n5
Brody, David, 93–94, 131n23
Brooks, Peter, 109–10
Brown, Darryl, 122n63
Brown, Michael, 78
Brueland, Harold, 109
Bull (television show), 129n40
Bundy, Ammon, 7–8, 107–8
Bundy, Cliven, 7–8, 107–8
Bureau of Justice, 10
Burnett, D. Graham, 48
Burns, Robert, 12, 43–44, 120n39, 123n12, 124n5, 124n7, 126n38
Bushel case, 30, 43–44, 83
Butler, Judith, 54–56
Butler, Paul, 95–96, 132n40

California, 8
Camden (New Jersey), 7, 19, 105
capital punishment, 8, 27, 82, 104
Central Intelligence Agency (CIA), 114–15
Central Park 5, 108, 110; and bias, 109; false confessions, 112; faulty narrative, 109; media coverage, 133n27; and racism, 111
Chambers, Simone, 125n21
Chesterton, G. K., 14
Christianity, 19
citizenship, 2, 4, 6, 10–11, 16, 88, 91, 97–98, 101, 116; culture of, 99; denial of, 5; and punishment, 3, 12, 16, 102–4, 118n10; radical enfranchisement, as type of, 81
civic culture, 22
civic education, 2–3, 6